BEADS and SEQUINS
THE LEWISCRAFT STORY

BEADS and SEQUINS
THE LEWISCRAFT STORY

Paul Woods

DEDICATIONS

It's not often one finds a combination of caring, integrity, hard work and honesty in one person, let alone two. To have those two people find each other and stay together for more than 50 years is even more uncommon.

It is that special combination that allowed our mom and dad to build not only a successful family but also a successful business – Lewiscraft.

We are so pleased to have been able to work with our friend Paul Woods to tell the story of Lewiscraft. It is such an important part of our family's history and has touched the lives of so many Canadian crafters.

Thanks, Mom and Dad, for all you have done for us and our family. We love you very much.

—Melinda and Gord Lewis

To Eileen Woods, who made countless wall-mounted plaques using Lewiscraft's découpage materials in the 1970s. To Isabella (Grandma) Linton, who regularly made a beeline for the Lewiscraft store in London's Westmount Mall. And to the tens of thousands of store clerks and customers across Canada for whom crafting with Lewiscraft was much more than a hobby.

—Paul Woods

Copyright © Paul Woods

All rights reserved. No part of this publication may be reproduced or transmitted in any form or by any means, electronic or mechanical, including scanning, photocopying, recording or any information storage and retrieval system, without permission in writing from the Publisher, except by a reviewer or journalist who wishes to quote brief passages in a review or feature article.

Library and Archives Canada Cataloguing in Publication
Woods, Paul, 1957-, author
Beads and sequins: The Lewiscraft story / Paul Woods.
ISBN 978-1-365-21795-1 (paperback)
1. Lewiscraft – History. 2. Family-owned business enterprises – Canada. 3. Craft shops – Canada. 4. Stores, Retail – Canada. 5. Handicraft industries – Canada. I. Title.
HD9999.H364L49 2016   338.7'6174550971   C2016-904792-X

Design: Hartley Millson
Front cover photos: Top - Shutterstock/Low Sugar; Bottom - Shutterstock/Elena Rodalis
Back cover photo: Photos on back cover and interior cover: Richard Lautens

Table of Contents

Introduction 5
Cast of Characters 9
Over My Dead Body 11
Birth of an Empire 19
A "We" Person 27
Better Than Bare Feet 37
Miss Hamill 49
President in Waiting 55
Do It Yourself 63
The Balls to Be Good 73
Canada's Craft Catalogue 81
Dropping a Stitch or Two 93
Stealing Phone Books 97
Stack It High and Watch 'em Buy 105
Know When to Fold 115
In the Nick of Time 123
Boys' Club 129
So Long, Farewell 143
A Family Affair 147
Love Letters 155
Lewiscraft's Homes 162
Acknowledgements 166
About the Author 167

INTRODUCTION

To the best of my recollection, I never set foot in a Lewiscraft store. There was one in the shopping centre closest to my family's home (Westmount Mall in London, Ontario), but my trips there were generally focused on its record store, a source for new vinyl releases by Roxy Music or Bruce Springsteen.

I wasn't the least bit interested in making crafts, either. But my mom was. Lewiscraft catalogues were always tucked in with the newspapers and magazines in our living room on Jason Crescent. My mom made regular trips to the Lewiscraft store at Westmount to buy the materials she needed for craft projects. One of her favourite pastimes in the mid-1970s was putting together "plaques" – little slabs of plaster on which pictures from greeting cards were appliquéd.

It was only through this book project that I learned the craft she did was called découpage, and the key to its success was a Lewiscraft glue/sealer named Podgy.

The first time I heard the word "Podgy" was in October of 2013, over lunch with a colleague and friend, Gord Lewis. I had known Gord for more than a dozen years at that point. In his role as an executive with Proteus Performance Management, he had served as governance and investment adviser to two company-sponsored pension plans for which I held fiduciary responsibilities. He and I stayed in touch after I left the company that sponsored those pension plans in 2011.

Aside from catching up with one another, there was a small purpose for our lunch that day in Toronto's Yorkville district. Gord wanted me to sign a copy of the book I had recently published (*Bouncing Back: From National Joke to Grey Cup Champs*, the story of the 1981-83 Toronto Argonauts). He had previously gone online to purchase a copy for himself; now he planned to give a copy to a friend who was a big fan of the Canadian Football League, and he wanted me to inscribe it.

As we chatted, Gord mentioned he had always wanted someone to write the history of his family's business, Lewiscraft. I had been dimly aware of his connection to the company – at one point before a pension meeting years earlier, he had made an offhand comment that prompted me to say something like, "Wait a minute – you mean you're Lewis of Lewiscraft?"

Now he was telling me the story of Lewiscraft – how it had begun with a leather sales representative (Gord's great-grandfather Ed Lewis), evolved into a mail-order business (under his grandfather Gerry Lewis) and then become a major retailer, with stores from coast to coast (under his father, Gary Lewis). Gord had at one time thought he might become the fourth member of the Lewis family to run the business, but his dad had sold it in 1995 (a decision, he emphasized, he wholeheartedly supported).

It was a subject that seemed ripe for what I had done with *Bouncing Back*: a journalistic endeavour involving a review of archival material and interviews with individuals connected to the story.

From that conversation came this book. I committed to research and write the story of Lewiscraft – provided that Gord's dad was willing to participate in the project. A similar plan had apparently been undertaken several years earlier, but Gary Lewis had decided it wasn't a good idea, and the project had fizzled. So one of my first tasks was to meet with Gary (and his charming wife, Eleanore) to win their trust and support. They embraced the idea with enthusiasm, and immediately started telling me entertaining stories about the business and the family's involvement in it.

Still, I was worried it would not be an easy book to research and write. As noted above, I knew nothing about crafting or the company at the outset (whereas the story I told in *Bouncing Back* was one to which I had a deep personal connection as a diehard fan of the Argos).

Gord gave me a manuscript of an earlier effort at documenting Lewiscraft's history. It had been undertaken in the mid-1990s by Evelyn Hamill, a long-time executive of the company, at the family's instigation. Packed with facts, it was (to put it mildly) dry. How could I possibly bring this story to life?

I needn't have worried. Once I started interviewing people associated with Lewiscraft – starting with members of the Lewis family, then expanding to executives and store clerks and customers – it became evident this was a story rich in potential, and bursting to be told. A story about business, about history, about Canadian society. A story about fascinating characters.

A story about a company to which thousands of Canadians (mostly, but not exclusively, women and girls) felt a deep attachment – and in many cases still do, nearly a decade after it disappeared, and two decades after the Lewis family's involvement ended. As Shirley Sano, Lewiscraft's art director from 1978 to 1995, told me, "Whenever I tell anybody what I used to do, nine out of ten women will say, 'Oh, I loved Lewiscraft.'"

I've experienced similar reactions when I've told people I was working on this book. A lot of Canadians, it seems, loved Lewiscraft. *Beads and Sequins* is for the women and men who built the company, and for those who bought its products, made its crafts – and might even still have a bottle of Podgy.

Notes about attribution

One of the challenges that comes with writing about a family-owned business is figuring out how to identify multiple members of the family who share the same last name. While it is customary in journalism to identify speakers by their last names after they are initially introduced ("says Lewis"), doing so in this book would have made it difficult for readers to keep track of who was speaking. Consequently, I have generally used first names for members of the Lewis family after first reference ("Gary remembers"), although all are identified in full within each chapter. On occasion I used both first and last names on subsequent reference, if it seemed appropriate to do so for clarity.

For convenience and consistency, I have also chosen to use present-tense attribution ("says" rather than "said") for all comments made by individuals I interviewed for Beads and Sequins. *This includes Janet Campbell, who, sadly, died about a year after I interviewed her in 2014.*

CAST OF CHARACTERS

Edward (Ed) Lewis (1877-1943): Founder of the company that became Lewiscraft

Gerald (Gerry) Lewis (1904-1996): Eldest son of Ed and Alice Lewis; second president of the company

Gladys Lewis: Gerry's wife

Gary Lewis: Only son of Gerry and Gladys Lewis; third president of the company

Eleanore Lewis: Gary's wife

Herb Lewis: Gerry's brother; killed in action during the Second World War, he had been expected by Gerry and others to play an important role in the company

Fred, Bill, Ivy and Ethel Lewis: Gerry's other siblings; all worked at times in the business, but only Bill held a long-term position

Alec Coutie: Son of Gladys Lewis's brother; he worked closely alongside Gary Lewis in senior roles with Lewiscraft

Lynda (Henry), Laura and Gord Lewis: Children of Gary and Eleanore; Lynda and Gord both spent several years in various roles with Lewiscraft; Gord was in line to become the fourth member of the Lewis family to run the company until it was sold by his father

Evelyn Hamill: Worked at Lewiscraft from 1937 until 1978, in a variety of senior roles; known universally as Miss Hamill; she was thought to have been in love with Herb Lewis before he was killed in action

Mary Ohorodnyk: Secretary/executive assistant to three generations of Lewises: Gerry, Gary and Gord

Shirley Sano: Lewiscraft's art director from 1978 to 1995; responsible for the look and feel of the company as demonstrated in its annual catalogues

Janet Campbell: A senior Lewiscraft executive responsible for marketing and operations starting in the mid-1970s

Bob Gatfield: Campbell's husband; the company's chief financial officer for two decades

Tricia Cadieux: Managed several Lewiscraft stores and also served as a district manager

Louise Chapdelaine: Held a variety of positions, including district manager and director of purchasing, in a 31-year career at Lewiscraft

Mary Mackie: Worked in several stores and eventually became head of merchandising

Sandra Massey: Head of design at Lewiscraft's head office

Kim Schell: Senior executive who managed Lewiscraft's district managers

Mona Kleperis: An artist who worked under Shirley Sano

Mark Mattin: Worked as a clerk in several Toronto-area Lewiscraft stores in the 1970s

Mary Breen: Worked as a sales clerk in Lewiscraft stores in west Toronto and Mississauga

Bruce Pearson: Served as a business consultant and adviser to Gerry and Gary Lewis

Eddie Black: Scion of the Blacks Photo family; put together a group to purchase Lewiscraft from Gary Lewis in 1995; ousted as president eighteen months later

John Wilcox: One of the two main investors in the Westock group that purchased Lewiscraft in 1995; chief executive officer and primary owner through the company's final decade of existence

David Demchuk: Lifelong crafter, Lewiscraft fan and one-time author of a blog called Knit Like a Man

Chapter 1
OVER MY DEAD BODY

It seemed like just another day at the office for Gary Lewis – until his father uttered a few words that would change things forever.

Gerry Lewis was president of a company that bore his name (Gerry Lewis Ltd.) but was known to Canadian crafters as Lewiscraft. And on September 22, 1969, Gary's thirty-fifth birthday, Gerry announced that he was retiring and turning the business over to his son.

Gary was not greeted with fanfare when he broke the news to his wife, Eleanore. She was visiting with a couple of friends when Gary arrived from the office.

"He came in and said, 'By the way, Dad made me president.' The three of us all turned and said, 'That's nice.'"

"Nobody gave a damn what the hell I said," Gary says with a wry smile. "It just went over their head – nobody cared."

Eleanore, though, says the nonchalant response was based on a belief that Gary was simply fulfilling his destiny. "We all cared. But the thing is, we all just thought that was a given."

Gary, too, thought it was more or less a given. Since joining Lewiscraft full-time after graduating from Ryerson Polytechnic Institute in 1957, he had both hoped and assumed he would eventually run the company his grandfather started in 1913.

Still, though, there was potential for his father's shadow to loom large. Gerry Lewis may have been retiring, but he wasn't planning to stop working. In fact, he would continue to go into the office every day (except during parts of the winter, when he was in Florida) for another twenty-five years.

And so it was with a curious mixture of determination, confidence and dread that Gary approached his father a few weeks after he took over the business.

The company had been in the Lewis family since Gerry's father, Ed Lewis, struck out on his own as a sales representative to the Ontario shoe trade more than half a century earlier. Gerry had become president in 1944 after his father died. Gary joined the business in 1957 and had learned the ropes by working in a variety of roles over the past dozen years.

Now, here in the fall of 1969, the enterprise was Gary's to run. He had just made his first big decision.

And Gerry wasn't going to like what Gary was about to tell him.

The story of Lewiscraft is a story of a company that transformed itself several times over nine decades. Starting as a leather wholesale business in 1913 supplying shoemakers, it developed a rudimentary retail operation during the Great Depression, selling bits of scrap leather to Torontonians looking to stitch together wallets and other small personal items at low cost.

During the Second World War, the company was commissioned by the Canadian government to supply craft materials to rehabilitation hospitals where wounded soldiers were sent for occupational therapy.

After the war, a mail-order business was established. Canadians would fill in an order form, send in a couple of bucks and get back small kits with all the elements needed to make personal crafts: bags of beads, sticks of glue, pieces of leather and so on.

For a decade or so beginning in the mid-1950s, the primary financial driver for Lewiscraft was a make-your-own moccasin kit known as "Make-a-Moc." Once that craze – which spread to the United Kingdom as well as across Canada – died down, other craft items supplanted it.

The mail-order business continued to grow. Lewiscraft surpassed $1 million in annual sales for the first time in 1968.

A year later, Gerry turned the presidency over to his son. And Gary Lewis had new-fangled ideas about where to take the enterprise.

He was going to start opening retail stores – which required a willingness to stand up to his father.

To Gerry Lewis, selling Lewiscraft's products in stores was a ticket to failure.

In addition to the store attached to the company's warehouse at 284 King Street West in downtown Toronto, Gerry had, in the late 1940s, opened a

Lewis Craft Supplies store in Saint John, New Brunswick, circa 1950

stand-alone Toronto store at 645 Yonge Street, a few blocks south of Bloor Street. Stores were opened soon after in Winnipeg (on Graham Avenue), and Saint John, New Brunswick (on Water Street).

None of the stores produced a bonanza of revenue, and the two outside Toronto eventually ran into issues beyond their control: a doubling of rent for the Winnipeg store and a refusal by the Saint John landlord to renew the lease. Less than a decade after the first stand-alone store opened, all three were shuttered and Lewiscraft returned its focus almost exclusively to its mail-order business, plus the small retail store at the warehouse.

"The stores flunked," says Gary. "It wasn't such a good idea at the time, and I think it just about put the company under."

It was in that context that Gary went to break the news to the man who had opened – and then closed – the three stores two decades earlier.

I'm going to open a store, he told his dad.

"Over my dead body," replied Gerry.

Gary was undeterred. And Gerry, despite opposing the idea, was not prepared to pull rank or overrule his son. Even though he planned to keep coming to work, the man who had transformed Lewiscraft from a leather wholesale business into one of Canada's most prominent consumer mail-order suppliers was not a guy who would interfere with his progeny.

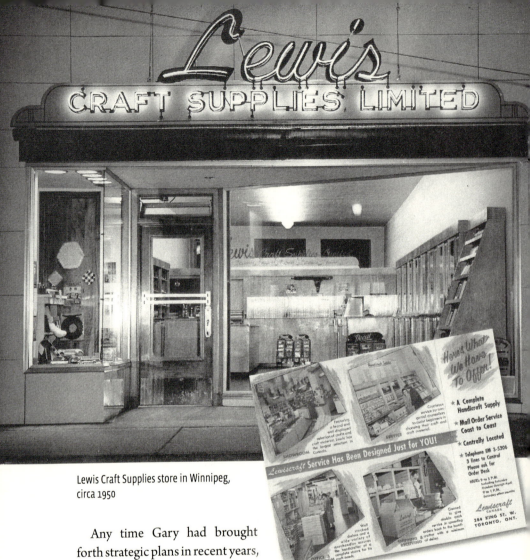

Lewis Craft Supplies store in Winnipeg, circa 1950

Any time Gary had brought forth strategic plans in recent years, Gerry had been receptive. And he wasn't about to get in the way after the change in leadership. "Once he turned it over, he literally turned it over the next day," his son recalls.

The company was now Gary's to run as he saw fit.

Gary and his cousin and right-hand man, Alec Coutie, had been plotting a move back into retail even before the transfer of power. They had noted with growing interest that a new method of retailing had been rolling across the country since the early 1960s.

Shopping malls, mostly in the suburbs, were opening in every city. With the economy flourishing and the Baby Boom roaring through the post-war years, subdivisions had sprung up far from city centres. Folks living in the 'burbs weren't as inclined as the previous generation to do their shopping on Main Street. And with every household having at least one car, getting to a mall was easy. The malls, featuring one or two "anchor" department stores and dozens of smaller specialty retailers, became a focal point for shopping as well as hanging out.

The country's first enclosed shopping centre had opened in 1950 in West Vancouver, British Columbia. The massive Yorkdale Shopping Centre opened in Toronto in 1964, and other malls were springing up from one coast to the other.

"You've got to get to where the people are," says Gary. "The consumer was starting to change the way they would buy. They were going to the shopping centres. So we figured maybe what we should do is to try to put a store in a shopping centre.

"We analyzed and concluded that if we were going to survive, we couldn't just stay in the mail order business; we would have to go into retail.

"Long term, mail order was not going to survive because people wanted instant satisfaction – they wanted the convenience of getting their stuff instantly. They didn't want to put an order in the mail and wait for the parcel to come."

Aside from that, there was an essential link in the mail-order chain that the business could not control. And it had already had a negative impact.

Four years earlier, postal workers across Canada had staged an illegal "wildcat" strike. Workers in the public service at that time were forbidden to strike, but the "posties" walked off the job anyway.

One of the primary outcomes of that dispute was new legislation allowing unionized federal employees to strike if collective bargaining broke down. Sure enough, in 1968 the first legal strike of postal workers was called, with letter carriers and sorters staying off the job for twenty-two days.

This was a full two decades before private courier services like Purolator and FedEx became viable alternatives to postal delivery. For companies such as Lewiscraft that relied on the mail to receive payment and deliver goods, an end to postal service choked off cash flow, temporarily crippling the operation.

Consequently, Gary was determined to find a more direct way to reach consumers.

Gary Lewis, 1971

In that regard, his story and indeed the story of the modern era of Lewiscraft bear a more than passing resemblance to that of another entrepreneur: Richard Branson. Four and a half decades ago, both Lewis and Branson were confounded in their efforts to successfully execute corporate strategy because of occurrences outside their control: postal strikes.

Branson is the flamboyant founder of the UK-based Virgin Group Ltd., which at various times has included music megastores, air and rail travel, hotels, mobile communications, finance, retail, alcohol and leisure companies. But back in the late 1960s and early 1970s, he – like Gary Lewis – ran a fairly simple business that sold its wares, and brought in most of its revenue, by mail.

Branson had founded Virgin to sell vinyl records through mail order at prices that undercut traditional storefront retailers. Lewiscraft had evolved over the years into a catalogue sales operation, with customers (mostly women) across Canada sending in a few dollars at a time in exchange for mail delivery of craft products, from candle-making components to rug-hooking kits.

And both Richard Branson and Gary Lewis learned the hard truth that a mail-order business is entirely dependent on a fully functioning postal delivery system.

In Branson's case, a strike by British postal workers in 1971 prompted him to phase out mail-order record sales and move into storefront retailing, starting what evolved into the Virgin empire.

In Lewis's case, disruptions to mail delivery were a recent and bitter memory just as he was getting used to the idea that Lewiscraft was now his business to run.

A vigourous and healthy but humble and low-key man in his early eighties, Gary still sees red when he thinks back on the way Canadian postal workers "used to love to go on strike.

"We would have a catalogue come out in September and those guys would go on strike at the end of September and just about put us out of business.

"Since that day, I've had a grudge against the post office."

Lewiscraft still had its original store, at its warehouse in downtown Toronto. Located near the corner of King and John streets just north of where the CN Tower now stands, it was dingy and dusty, with a creaky wooden floor, a musty odour and a dumbwaiter to transport goods from upstairs in the warehouse. "It was really medieval," says Mary Mackie, who worked as a buyer for Lewiscraft.

And it wasn't anything like the mall stores to which Canadians were flocking.

Gary negotiated a deal to open a store in Scarborough, at the intersection of Victoria Park and Sheppard avenues. It was in a strip mall rather than an enclosed centre, but the price was right. However, the developer couldn't make the space available in compliance with the contract, and Gary was able to get out of the deal. "It was the best thing we ever did."

Rather than wedging itself into a soulless strip mall, the first Lewiscraft store opened in a three-year-old indoor shopping centre: Agincourt Mall,

Beads and Sequins: The Lewiscraft Story

Gerry Lewis, undated

at Kennedy Road and Sheppard Avenue in Scarborough. "Nov. 23, 1969, at 10:30 in the morning," is Lewis's startlingly precise recollection of the opening.

Two months to the day after he had been named president of Lewiscraft, and just in time for customers to start buying supplies for Christmas crafts. Pent-up demand was evident: people lined up to get in the store on Day 1.

The first piece of what was to become a retail empire was now in place.

But the story actually began more than half a century earlier...

Chapter 2
BIRTH OF AN EMPIRE

Wander around a small sliver of lower Toronto streets, from Jarvis along Front to Yonge and up a block to Wellington, and you'll see a couple of gorgeous pieces of the city's past. On the eastern edge of this roughly four-square-block patch of land there's the stately, imposing presence of St. Lawrence Market, part of which dates back to 1845. A block away, there's the red-brick, triangular Gooderham Building, commonly known as the Flatiron, poking out towards Church Street at the point where Front and Wellington converge. It's stood since 1892.

Other than that, though, there isn't much that screams out "history." And there's nothing at all that tells you this tiny chunk of Toronto was home, a century ago, to a thriving trade in locally made shoes – and the first home of the enterprise that came to be known as Lewiscraft.

Just west of the Flatiron building (which now houses a just-like-all-the-others Firkin pub below ground) is a small public park, frequently used as a location shoot for movies and TV series. Gone without a trace is the Flatiron's former next-door neighbour, the Frontwell Building.

In that building – in a basement space, to be precise – a young businessman named Edward Richard Lewis struck out on his own back in 1913.

Young Lewis was the second son of Alfred James Lewis and his wife, the former Mary Anne Elderton. Alfred had emigrated from Wales around the time of Canadian Confederation and happened to meet Mary Anne, a governess in England and Ireland who had come to the new land in the service of Viscount Charles Stanley Monck of Ballytrammon, first Governor-General of the new Dominion of Canada.

Miss Elderton and Mr. Lewis were married two years after their new country was born. They settled in Barrie, north of Toronto, where Alfred

Ed Lewis, circa 1913

worked as a building contractor. Two sons came along – Llewellyn Alfred in 1875 and Edward Richard two years later. Llewellyn grew up to become an apprentice printer in Barrie, then moved to Toronto where he spent the rest of his career working on the printing presses of the *Toronto Daily Star*.

As a young man, Edward couldn't seem to find a niche for himself at first. He spent some time selling groceries and decorating houses, and eventually heeded his brother's advice to move to Toronto, the thriving provincial capital. There his life took the turn that eventually led to the creation of Lewiscraft.

Ed got hired into a junior position with A.R. Clarke & Co. Ltd., which operated a sheepskin tannery and leather production factory on Eastern Avenue in the part of Toronto known as Leslieville. Clarke's sheepskin was used to insulate shoes and boots and in the manufacture of gloves, coats and other pieces of clothing.

Lewis quickly absorbed the intricacies of tanning, the process by which animal skins and hides are treated with tools and chemicals to produce

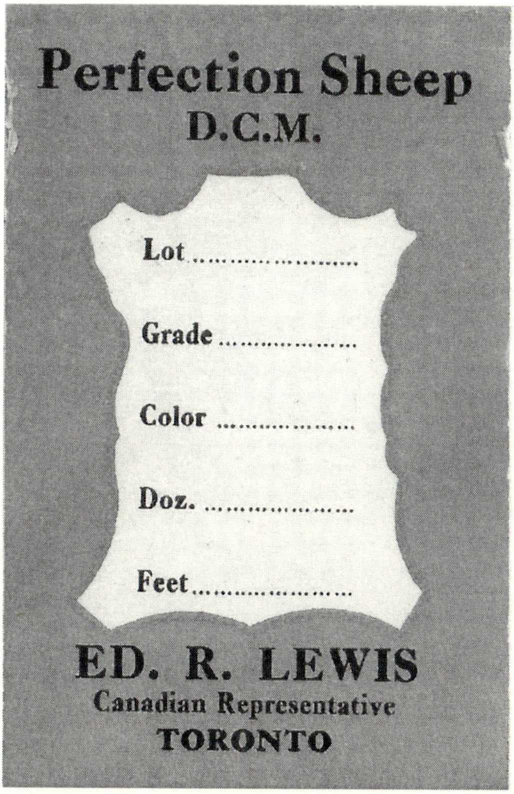

Perfection Sheep
D.C.M.

Lot..........................

Grade..........................

Color..........................

Doz...........................

Feet..........................

ED. R. LEWIS
Canadian Representative
TORONTO

Product tag for sheepskin distributed by Ed Lewis

durable and pliable leather. His expertise and experience led to an offer from another sheepskin outfit, H.B. Johnston Co. Ltd., to take charge of its tannery, located on Dundas Street where it meets the Don River.

Ed added sales to his responsibilities, peddling his firm's sheepskin to the shoemaking trade in Ontario, Quebec and Atlantic Canada. (Difficult as it may be to believe in this world of globalized trade and "made in China" labels, a century ago most shoes were manufactured not far from the folks who bought them.)

Driven to learn and succeed, Ed enrolled in business and French language courses – when he wasn't working six days a week, singing in the choir at All Saints Anglican Church or playing clarinet in the Reserve Army Band, that is. Speaking French would come in handy a few years later.

The Johnston tannery's owner, Harry Johnston, decided to expand into calfskin and cowhide tanning. Lewis, who had experience with cowhide at

Alice and Ed Lewis, with sons Gerald and Fred, circa 1910

A.R. Clarke and had acquired considerable knowledge of the industry on his sales calls, felt this move was a mistake. Two firms just north of Toronto, he knew, had the Canadian cowhide market cornered and in fact had so much business they were also exporting leather overseas.

Young Lewis, by this time married to the former Alice Maud Bennet and father to three sons, tried to help Johnston make a go of the expanded business. But he could not shake off his misgivings, and in 1913 he decided to resign his position at H.B. Johnston and hang out his own shingle.

Borrowing against his life insurance policy, taking out a second mortgage on his Rainford Road home and dipping into his own bank account, Ed obtained a line of credit from the Bank of Toronto and opened Ed. R. Lewis Ltd. – Tanners & Leather Supplies.

He found premises at 50 Front Street East, in the basement of the Frontwell Building near Wellington. Six steps down from the sidewalk, with just a single small window, the 1,800-square-foot office was certainly nothing to write home to Barrie about. But the rent was just twenty-five dollars per month, and it was right in the heart of the thriving shoe trade, with a dozen

The Lewis company's receiving department, 1940s

or more suppliers wedged into the two blocks between Scott Street and the St. Lawrence Market.

Lewis had a telephone installed (the number, in those days of scarce phones and named exchanges, was Main 2597). The space had a warehouse, with wooden shelving to hold bundles of leather and a large table to inspect incoming shipments.

A workshop had room to repair and maintain machines that measured leather, a service that Ed. R. Lewis Ltd. provided for other outfits in the vicinity. (An informal history of Lewiscraft, put together in the mid-1990s by Evelyn Hamill – whose name will appear again later in these pages – was succinct on the value of these contraptions: "The measuring machine is really the cash register for tanners and buyers of leather.")

One of Ed Lewis's secrets to staying in business was diversifying: constantly coming up with new ways to serve and attract customers. Taking note of a growing opportunity in the United States for tanners' agents and representatives, he reckoned he could offer such a service to tanners outside Toronto.

His first client was Duclos & Payan Ltd. of Saint-Hyacinthe, Que., a tanner that wanted to sell its leather into the burgeoning Ontario footwear trade. Lewis resumed studying French, by correspondence course, and became fluent enough to be entrusted by Duclos & Payan with handling their agency, sales and warehouse needs in Toronto.

Lewis Leather truck in the Bathurst Street yard, 1940s

The next opportunity to expand the offerings of Ed. R. Lewis Ltd. came from the United States. The company became Canadian sales representative for one of the largest sheepskin tanners south of the border. The wares of Donnell, Oarman & Mudge Inc. of Boston, especially grey suede sheepskin, became especially popular for lining women's shoes.

Lewis also sold small quantities of calfskin, kidskin and occasionally snakeskin to custom shoemakers.

The company expanded beyond leather – "tried anything that would provide work," Evelyn Hamill's informal history reported. Filling small plastic tubes with household cement from five-gallon containers was one of the small sidelight businesses that kept revenue flowing in the early years. Another idea saw small bits of scrap leather fashioned into lid fasteners on Thermos bottles.

The Second World War led to the creation of some products used in service, including binocular covers, leather reinforcements for canvas shoes and anklets, and felt covers for gas tanks on Mosquito bombers. Packing cases built to ship airplane motors were later re-sold as dog houses or used for storage in Lewis's warehouse yard.

The creation of an "obsolete leather" department was another innovation: its mission was to dispose of scrap leather accumulated by shoemakers and leather suppliers. Those outfits didn't want the stuff piling up and would pay Lewis to haul it away. "At times, the pile of upper leather scrap in the centre of the yard looked like a small mountain," Hamill wrote.

Lewis also established a small mail-order business – a precursor to what Lewiscraft would become in the 1950s and '60s.

But the biggest change to the early operation of Ed. R. Lewis Ltd. was its entry into the market for homemade leather crafts. Tanneries weren't interested in serving the needs of individuals – but Lewis was. So a handicraft division was created.

Men and women would stop by the Lewis facility to buy small quantities of leather that could be fashioned into billfolds, purses, comb cases and the like. Some of this leather would be scrap from the suppliers who had been only too happy to have Lewis get rid of it for them. Lewis would cut much of it into smaller pieces and sell it off to crafters – getting paid on the way in and the way out.

As the company grew, it had to move several times in the early years – initially into larger premises in the city's leather district near the St. Lawrence Market, then to a warehouse on King Street West near John Street.

The end of a five-year lease on King Street forced another move just as the Second World War was breaking out in 1939. The company was finally doing well enough to justify purchasing a property of its own. Ed Lewis found what he needed at 8 Bathurst Street, just south of Old Fort York.

On land rented from Canadian Pacific Railways, he purchased a group of metal-clad buildings and a brick structure for the grand total of $5,000. (Nowadays no building stands where the Lewis premises were located; the Gardiner Expressway runs overhead.) The facilities were spartan and needed constant attention to keep hot water running, but they belonged to Ed. R. Lewis Ltd.

As the company expanded, it was becoming a family affair. Ed and Alice's eldest son, Gerald – known to all as Gerry – joined in 1924 at age 20. Second son Fred came on board four years later, and in 1938 they were joined by a third son, Herb, as well as two brothers-in-law, Herb Vince and David Coutie.

The fortunes of the company – and the family – would change dramatically in the span of 367 days. On Jan. 7, 1943, Ed Lewis died suddenly at the

Staff members in 1942, including Fred Lewis (far left), Evelyn Hamill (third from left), Ed Lewis (fourth from left) and Gerry Lewis (sixth from right)

age of 65, leaving the company owned (but not operated) by his widow. All hands strove to continue on as Ed would have wished, but this represented a massive turn in fortune. The man who had built the enterprise from humble beginnings three decades earlier was suddenly gone.

Exactly one month after the founder's death, tragedy struck. Herb, who in 1941 had enlisted in the Royal Canadian Air Force and trained as a bomber pilot, was shot down and declared missing on Feb. 7, 1943. He was officially declared dead six months later. According to Evelyn Hamill's informal history of Lewiscraft, Herb "was to have been the future star of the company." In later years his brother, Gerry, would sometimes hang his head and say how much he missed Herb. Clearly Herb's death was a loss to the company as well as to the family.

The founder was dead. The future star was gone. And the run of bad fortune continued. On Jan. 9, 1944, barely a year after her husband's death, Alice Lewis died.

A new era was about to begin.

Chapter 3
A "WE" PERSON

Gerry Lewis, who turned a ragtag collection of small business units into one of Canada's biggest mail-order operations under the banner of Lewiscraft, was a creature of habit. In fact, he wore the same blue suit in the office every day – for three decades. He believed in protocol and fostered traditional values of respect and teamwork.

"He was kind of like Mister Rogers," recalls Lynda Henry, who worked alongside her grandfather for several years. "He would walk in with his suit coat on, take his suit coat off, hang it on the coat rack, get his work suit coat on and sit down.

"There was a boy who worked in the warehouse on King Street – he had long sideburns and my grandfather didn't want to talk to him. He was incredibly progressive in his thinking with regards to business and change and adapting to what was in front of him, yet he still didn't like it if someone had long sideburns.

"There were some things that just weren't going to change about him. Very old-fashioned in some respects."

Indeed, Gerry had old-fashioned values. He believed that a deal was sealed with a handshake. That if he said something, he meant it. That employees should enter the office through the staff entrance, reserving the front door for customers and suppliers. That a man should never leave his cap on when sitting down to a meal.

And that the company president was on the same level as the most junior employee in the warehouse.

Gerry always said "he was the chief bottle washer and sweeper," remembers his grandson, Gord Lewis. "Even in his late 80s, he'd walk around and say, 'I'm just sweeping the floors.'"

Gerry Lewis, 1928

Those homespun values were forged over a career that encompassed seventy of the eighty-three years the Lewis family owned and operated the company. Gerry joined as a sales representative working for his dad in 1924, at the age of 21, and hung up his blazer for the last time in 1994, a year before his son sold Lewiscraft.

We will never know why Alice Lewis chose to leave seventy-five per cent of Ed. R. Lewis Ltd. to Gerry, the eldest son in a family with six children, but there's little doubt she made the right decision. Gerry was driven to make the business succeed and grow. His surviving siblings – Fred, Bill, Ivy and Ethel – either had no interest or lacked Gerry's drive.

"His mother was the one who chose him to run the business," says Eleanore Lewis, Gerry's daughter-in-law. "She saw he was the brother that could handle it. He really did not want to let her down."

Gerry's son, Gary Lewis, says his father "was the only guy with any smarts or ability. She recognized that Dad was the one that would have the ability to do it. Dad had the work ethic and the ability to do things."

Fred, to whom Alice bequeathed twenty-five per cent of the company, had played a big role in the establishment of the handicraft division in the late 1930s. But he "didn't have a business mind at all," says Gary. "He was a little flighty. And his brother Bill – a nice, nice person, but no idea how to run a business. Whereas Dad knew how." Sisters Ethel and Ivy, meanwhile, held relatively minor roles with the company over the years.

One of the first challenges Gerry faced after being handed the reins of the Ed. R. Lewis Ltd. leather company was a set of draconian tax provisions aimed at preventing Canadian businesses from making "excess profits" during the Second World War. The federal Department of Munitions and Supply was ordering a lot of leather products and materials from Lewis (some of it for use in land-mine covers), but was taxing at a usurious rate that made it just about impossible to make money.

To get around this unsustainable tax burden, Gerry managed to negotiate the right to start a new company – something generally forbidden during the war effort. The revenue could then be spread over two companies and taxed at a manageable rate. So in 1944, Lewiscraft Art Supplies Ltd. was formed as a subsidiary of Ed. R. Lewis Ltd., and took over its handicrafts division.

The Lewis companies had accounts at the Bank of Nova Scotia – until some bad experiences with a supervisor there triggered a move to Dominion Bank (which later merged with the Bank of Toronto to form what is now known as TD Bank). Playing on the name Bank of Nova Scotia, "he always called them the 'bank of no soap,'" says Gary. "He never forgave them," adds Eleanore.

Despite the responsibilities of running a company, Gerry remained a salesman at heart. In 1946 he formed Gerry Lewis Ltd. as the holding company for Ed. R. Lewis Leather, Lewiscraft Art Supplies and other subsidiaries

engaged in non-leather business (such as distribution of chemicals and glues).

Just as Ed Lewis had been an agent for leather companies selling to the shoe trade, Gerry also promoted products made by other companies. Advertisements in Footwear Journal for Dewey & Almy Chemical Co. featured Lewis as the Toronto representative of Darex cement, "the kind shoe men like to work with."

Lewis spent much of his time on the road, visiting the shoemakers of Ontario – which by the mid-1940s were mostly clustered around Galt, Hespeler and Preston (now Cambridge), southwest of Toronto.

"He'd take the train on Sunday night and get there on Monday morning, come back on Friday, work in the office on Saturday and then Sunday he'd take the train again," remembers Gary. "Then he'd be gone all week again.

"I really didn't have a holiday with Dad until I was 16. He didn't take holidays."

Gary's daughter Lynda describes her grandfather as "a product of 1904. He left school at quite a young age; I think he had a Grade 8 education.

"But he wasn't afraid to work, and he worked really hard. He worked six, sometimes seven days a week. That Protestant work ethic. He worked a lot, went on the road a lot – it was his life."

The elder Lewis expected his progeny to follow suit.

"I worked at Bathurst Street all through the summers," says Gary. "Loading freight cars with scrap leather, or standing eight hours a day on a clicker, clicking out links for link belts.

"We had a time clock, and one day at 5 o'clock everybody was standing

Brampton tannery staff, late 1940s

around ready to punch the clock. I was out there with them. Dad came along and said, 'I don't want to ever see you standing there at 5 o'clock to punch out. You don't quit – you just keep going.'"

Gord Lewis, Gary's son, has a similar story from his time working for Lewiscraft as a young man, when Gerry was still going into the office each day.

"My work day typically ended around 6 p.m. One day I was leaving – I don't remember what time it was, but I wasn't the last one leaving – say it was 5 o'clock. My grandfather saw me packing up and said, 'When did you join the union?'"

While that comment was a good-natured but serious-minded jab at his grandson, it also reflected Gerry's fierce determination to keep unions out of the Lewis family business. Shortly after purchasing a tannery in Brampton, west of Toronto, in 1946, Lewis faced a crisis. The story was recounted in an informal history of the company written in the mid-1990s by longtime employee Evelyn Hamill:

"The initial visit to the plant, after finalizing the transaction, was a disaster. The group was met by a union organizer who had convinced the staff that now was the time to organize. . . . This was a problem never before experienced.

"As a company that had always treated its people the best it could, Gerry Lewis Ltd. did not want outside interests trying to tell it how to be fair. . . . This unexpected reception required careful thinking and little comment at the time."

After deliberating, Lewis came up with a strategy that was both blunt and effective. The tannery was closed for "renovations and equipment overhaul."

This work lasted six weeks, long enough to ensure that the unionization effort was abandoned by the laid-off workers.

Once the tannery was reopened, some of its original employees ("who had not wanted to join the troublemakers in the first place," according to Hamill) were rehired.

"He always swore that he'd shut the place down before he'd ever let a union in," says Gord (who has since gone on to provide governance and financial advice to pension plans, several of which are administered jointly by a company and a union).

Successfully keeping the union out of the tannery did not mean exploiting its workers, though. In a 1951 booklet about the company issued to shareholders and suppliers, Gerry noted proudly that "our tannery workers were (among) the first in the Canadian tanning industry to receive two weeks' vacation with pay and to have every legal holiday honoured."

Gerry's opposition to unions might be seen as somewhat at odds with his general philosophy. He believed in treating everyone, at every level, with respect and courtesy. Those who knew him best – his family members, but also colleagues at Lewiscraft – say he never placed himself above others.

The elder Lewis made a point of walking through the office and warehouse every day, saying hi to everyone. "It literally was on his to-do list," says Gord, whose father followed suit when he became president. "Class warfare was never supported by my dad or my grandfather."

"He was a businessman, but very human," says Louise Chapdelaine, who worked for the company for 32 years. "He talked to everyone."

"He was very appreciative," says Bruce Pearson, an adviser to both Gerry and Gary Lewis in the 1960s and '70s. "He was always thanking you for something."

Lynda Henry says people who worked at Lewiscraft had a level of mutual respect that flowed directly from her grandfather. "He would always say, 'Lynder, you are no different just because your last name is the same as on the sign.' (To him) everybody was the same."

Laura Lewis, his other grand-daughter, adds that Gerry evaluated people on how they interacted with others. "He would say, 'They're a "we" person or they're a "me" person.' He really valued the sense that it was a team, it was a group, it wasn't about one person. He cared as much about the person that cleaned the building as the vice-president."

The 1951 booklet for shareholders and suppliers amplifies this point.

Block planing at Lewis's Bathurst Street operation, 1940s

Apparently written by Gerry himself – he is the only senior member of the organization not profiled – it is titled simply "Us":

> This may seem like a pretty short title to describe the events and people we have in mind. But it seems appropriate to sum up our group of companies and the folks that run them as just "us," which is our purpose in the following pages . . . so here we go for a talk about ourselves in plain language just as if we were having a fireside chat. . . .
> Our policy has always been to have with us the "get-ahead" type

Cutting lace in the Bathurst street facility, 1940s

of Canadian and as a result we are proud to point to the closely knit group that is moving us so steadily forward.

Perhaps we are not in the so-called "BIG Business" class but, after all, just being big is not everything worth striving for. Working along with friends to a common goal is surely a much better way to happiness and good living.

In the roll call of our company there are about eighty-five of "us." We don't just work for the group but **with** it, and that we know is our greatest insurance for the most successful kind of future. We are all self-made people who have come along the road by plenty of hard work and co-operation – without benefit of wealth or influence from the outside.

It is a tribute to "us" that our shareholders have appreciated the smooth, friendly working of our groups and by their thoughtfulness and loyalty have shown that they are as confident of our future as we are ourselves.

They know we are a "down-to-earth" organization with no pretense or extravagant ideas to hinder us. A good example of this is the fact that our head office is in reality a glorified garage. But it is not the outward appearance that counts with "us." As long as we have enough space in which to do our work, we can use the money right in the business instead of spending capital on expensive, high-flown modernizing....

It is doubtful whether any group of companies in Canada have a more efficient, younger age group than ours. This is a most important feature in any growing business for upon these young shoulders the long-term future operation of a company depends. We are certainly most fortunate to have men and women in each division who are able leaders of the sort that can get a job done without raising a lot of commotion and at the same time keep the best of relations with their co-workers.

We feel that this is one of the solid foundations on which our companies are built and want to give it special mention as we describe the present success of our business and explain why the prospects look so rosy for the future.

―――

Gerry's focus on building his team into a quasi-family was evident even after he finally retired for good in 1994. For more than forty years he had worked with a woman named Mary Ohorodnyk.

Gerry's executive assistant for much of that time, Ohorodnyk (pronounced oh-RODD-nick), was "a real lady," says Sandra Massey, who worked with her at Lewiscraft's head office.

"She always dressed as the perfect secretary. She never wore jeans. Always wore a dress." Traits that no doubt endeared her to the tradition-bound Gerry.

But now Gerry was retired, and his son, Gary, had sold the company. At the age of 60, Ohorodnyk feared she might be facing the axe. With no company pension to draw on, she had planned to keep working until she turned 65.

Ohorodnyk needn't have worried. Her job was safe, but even better news was to come one day shortly after the ownership change when Bob Gatfield,

"Us": The staff of Gerry Lewis Ltd. on the Bathurst Street lot, early 1950s

the company's head of finance, sauntered over to her desk and handed her an envelope.

Ohorodnyk opened it – and discovered that Gerry had, years earlier, opened a retirement savings plan in her name. The envelope contained a cheque for $87,000.

"He never told me," Ohorodnyk says with a touch of awe in her voice. "Shocked me. Lewiscraft had ended and the other company was taking over. This was on the books of the original Lewiscraft.

"I invested the money. I'm still living on it. I've got more money now than I ever had.

"He never told me."

Chapter 4
BETTER THAN BARE FEET

Day after day it piled up in the tannery. Stacks of raw, thick bullhide. Unsightly. Unsellable. Useless.

Gerry Lewis Ltd. was one of the few leather firms in Canada still buying and processing the hides of bulls. The bullhide was needed for Lewis's trademarked "Durabull" shoe sole leather, which the Savage Shoe Co. Ltd. of Galt, Ontario, one of Canada's largest producers, bought from Lewis for the soles on its children's footwear. But from each bullhide that was cut and tanned in Lewis's Brampton tannery, only a portion could be used to meet Savage's needs.

Large edges from the neck and belly were piling up, without any apparent value. Because the leather was heavy, buffing it for use on other products would be expensive.

But if there was one thing company president Gerry Lewis was good at, it was figuring out new products that people would want to buy.

"Gerry had an intuitively good merchant talent," remembers Bruce Pearson, a business adviser to the Lewis companies. "He could see something that would be saleable or attractive to a consumer. It could be something very small, like a roll of beads. He could see it – a very good merchant.

"He wasn't educated in a formal business sense, but he just had that good business eye. There were a lot of things he saw that he would have made a successful business out of, had he wanted to get involved."

An example of Gerry's ability to find new ways to make money had come during his decade as a Canadian sales rep for Dewey & Almy shoe glue, when he branched his business out to become Canadian distributor of a revolutionary process called Cryovac.

Developed in the 1940s, Cryovac involved putting meat in transparent plastic, removing the air with a vacuum pump and freezing the package.

Its slogan, "The second skin seals the flavour in," caught on as North America entered the age of suburbia, with new-fangled refrigerators and freezers pushing iceboxes into garbage dumps.

Lewis Specialties Ltd., one of five companies in the Lewis stable by 1951, served as Ontario distributor and national warehousing agent for Cryovac. The business eventually grew so large and complex that Lewis agreed to sell the contract to W.R. Grace & Co., which by then had acquired Dewey & Almy, for $15,000. Today Cryovac is sold around the world under the banner of Sealed Air Corp.

"It started being sold by Lewis Specialties in the basement of our King Street building, until it caught on," says Gerry's son, Gary. "That all started with Dad and W.R. Grace in our basement at King."

INSTANT CHASE & SANBORN OFFER!

Genuine "Lewiscraft"

MOCCASIN KIT

Yours for just

$2.00

with label from jar of Instant Chase & Sanborn (or panel from Bag or metal strip from tin of Chase & Sanborn Coffee).

• Finest top grain extra heavy bullhide
• Thick supple cushiony leather
• Pre-cut—just lace together
• Finest leather laces
• Sizes for all the family
• Men's, Boys' and Children's in natural retan finish
  —Women's and Girls' in Pearl Gray

ORDER FORM OTHER SIDE

A year or two later, with excess bullhide piling up at the Lewis tannery, a lightbulb went on inside the head of the "intuitively good merchant" Gerry Lewis. Why not use this piled-up bullhide by-product, instead of cowhide, to make moccasin kits?

The kits were already among Gerry Lewis Ltd.'s consumer product offerings. In the early 1950s, as the company was building up its mail-order business in the post-war economy, it had come into contact with a small business operated out of Winnipeg by a husband-and-wife team.

The couple had purchased the trade name "Make-a-Moc Kit" from a California firm, and were selling do-it-yourself moccasin kits using leather purchased from Gerry Lewis Ltd.

The moccasins were made from cowhide, with a sewn-on rubber sole. Customers would purchase the kit and stitch together the soles and uppers into comfortable, slipper-like moccasins.

The Winnipeg couple both had regular jobs; moccasins were something they marketed as a sideline. After determining they could not handle the volume of business they were generating, they approached Gerry Lewis Ltd. and its Lewiscraft subsidiary to buy them out. That mostly meant selling Lewis the right to market make-your-own moccasins under the "Make-a-Moc Kit" label.

Gerry bought up the couple's stock and the rights to the name for a few hundred dollars – thereby embarking on a venture that would, over the next decade, provide a tremendously successful revenue stream for Lewiscraft.

Sales were slow initially. Footwear in general was inexpensive, so the client base for moccasins was mostly intrepid do-it-yourselfers. And Lewis had to buy dies to punch out materials for all shoe sizes, so new production costs were added to the equation.

At the same time, the company was grappling with the oversupply of heavy leather from bullhide. That's when Gerry had the brainwave to use the bullhide for moccasin kits.

It made perfect sense, actually. The leather was already a golden tan colour, similar to the deerskin that North American indigenous peoples had used when they made their own moccasins, long before European settlers colonized and gained control over the continent.

The natural bull shoulder grain was prominent and showed imperfections, such as indentations from barbed wire the bulls had rubbed against. Shoe manufacturers would never accept such deviations from standard – but to customers making their own moccasins, these idiosyncratic marks were proof that the kits used genuine leather.

And so a new version of the moccasin kit was created. It was called a "sportsman type," with no insole or outsole – just leather stitched together by hand at home.

The 1954 Lewiscraft catalogue – the first to be done as a full magazine-style publication; fifty-two pages bound in heavy card stock and sold for twenty-five cents – featured "Foot comfort with Lewiscraft moccasins" on the inside cover. The accompanying description colourfully described the provenance of the leather:

"Each skin comes from Western Canada and Texas bulls. Once a raw bullhide is received at the Brampton tannery, a great deal of care goes into preserving the rugged natural top grain and the soft firmness of this fine leather. If you look closely at each moccasin, you will find right before your eyes actual tell-tale marks that meant big events in the life of one animal. Not

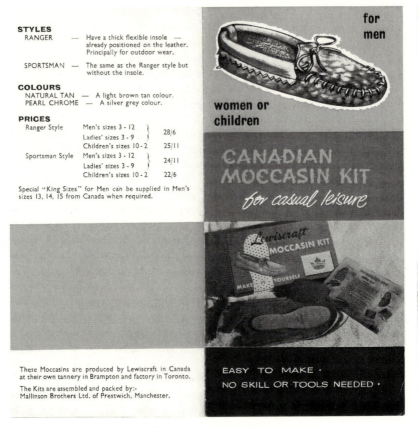

Promotional materials for Lewiscraft's moccasin kits, early 1960s

even barbed wire scratches, nor bite scars, are removed. In some cases, you might even see the sear marks left by man's branding iron . . . all as natural as natural can be!"

These new kits were sold at the company's retail outlets in Toronto, Winnipeg and Saint John, N.B., and to summer camps and Boy Scout troops. Then, in 1954, they became the centrepiece of a major marketing break for Gerry Lewis Ltd. and Lewiscraft.

A fellow named Jack Raymond was working for the J. Walter Thompson ad agency as an account executive for Standard Brands, a massive North American distributor of packaged food products. Standard was looking for a premium product to entice consumers to buy tins and bags of an instant coffee called Chase & Sanborn.

Raymond, a business acquaintance of Gerry's, thought the Lewiscraft

Make-a-Moc Kit might fit the bill. He pitched the idea to a senior executive at Standard Brands, who signed off on the idea. Standard created and distributed a coupon for buyers of Chase & Sanborn coffee products. "Genuine 'Lewiscraft' Moccasin Kit – Yours for just $2.00 with label."

Lewiscraft was about to go from relatively small sales of the moccasin kits into mass production.

Lewiscraft: A History, a document commissioned by Gary Lewis in the 1990s but never completed or published, explains the impact of this agreement between Lewis and Standard Brands: "It was like an impossible dream that came true at just the right time, when there was a mountain of leather piling up in the tannery."

Standard Brands ordered 20,000 kits. Almost immediately, coupons and the required Chase & Sanborn labels began flooding in to Lewiscraft.

Warehouse and factory staff were seconded to fill orders. Temporary typists had to be hired to process the coupons. (One of them, Mary Ohorodnyk, stayed with the company for almost five decades, ending up as a key administrative assistant to three generations of Lewises: Gerry, Gary and Gord.)

As recounted in *Lewiscraft: A History*, "this fine contract had moved almost 50,000 feet of leather, given a number of people work, and deposited cheques in the bank, something new for the company and the bank!"

The satisfied client, Standard Brands, later launched other promotions in partnership with Lewiscraft. Customers of Blue Bonnet margarine were offered red and blue plastic children's raincoats. Another promotion offered heavy English china cups in the shape of men's and women's heads.

Moccasins, meanwhile, became a steadily selling part of Lewiscraft's mail-order offerings to Canadian crafters. Gary Lewis, who did quasi-military training for two summers in the Canadian Officer Training Corps while attending Ryerson Polytechnic Institute, remembers "selling moccasin kits to all the guys in the platoons. I'd have them ship up cases of moccasins and I'd sell them.

"And we always had a booth at the Canadian National Exhibition and I'd be sitting there demonstrating, making moccasin kits. I must have made a million of those things."

Understanding even then the moccasin's place in the history of Lewiscraft, Gary held on to a kit, keeping it sealed in the plastic wrapper that would have come off the shop floor decades ago.

But the best was yet to come for Lewis's make-your-own moccasins. The casual footwear was to become a major part of the business.

In 1955, Lewiscraft had sold a pile of moccasin kits for use by Boy Scouts at a World Jamboree in Niagara-on-the-Lake, Ontario. Four years later, Gerry had another brainwave. On a hunch, he flew to England and took kit samples to Imperial Headquarters of the international Boy Scout movement. A scoutmaster bought 500 kits.

Gerry then found a commercial sales agent for England. Sales soon spread across the United Kingdom and into parts of Scandinavia, Germany, Holland and France. Production ramped up from 40,000 pairs in all of 1959 to 20,000 pairs a month in 1960, all assembled in the basement of Lewiscraft's warehouse on King Street West in Toronto.

By 1963, 50 years after Ed Lewis first went into the leather business as a one-man distribution operation serving the Ontario shoe trade, more than

Packaging for NeeBees, the Lewiscraft moccasin kit brand in England

300 outlets in England were selling Lewiscraft moccasin kits.

"Not just the scouts, but many a sedate Englishman now wants a pair of Canadian moccasins," Henk Hoppener reported in the *Financial Post* in 1960. A widespread belief had emerged in Europe, he wrote, that moccasins were "as much a part of Canadians' attire as wooden shoes (were)

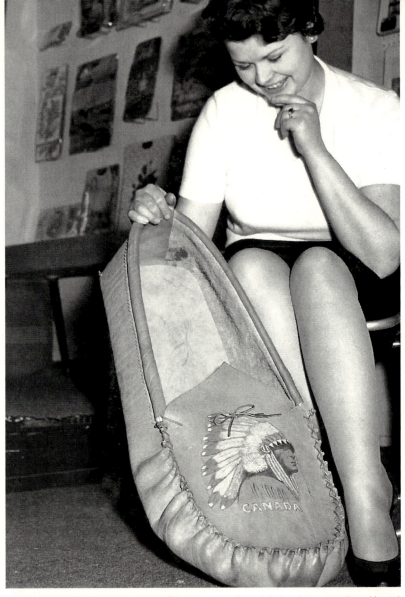

Mrs. P. Stott holding size-50 moccasin at Gifts and Fancy Goods Fair (Blackpool Gazette and Herald, 1969)

considered the traditional outfit of the Dutch."

Pearson, who worked with Lewiscraft as a business consultant starting in the early 1960s, has fond memories of the moccasin kits. His father, Harold Pearson, had served for many years as a director of Gerry Lewis Ltd. and at one time owned shares in the business.

"We all wore them. I wore them and Dad wore them. They were very comfortable. It was a very good business they had for a long time."

In 1965, while the musical British Invasion led by the Beatles was in full

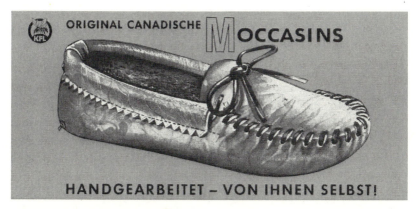

Moccasin kits were also peddled in Germany

swing across North America, the next phase of a Canadian business invasion began over 'ome with ready-made moccasins sold across England under the banner of NeeBees. The brand name was derived from the first names of the two "housewives" from Northern England who were peddling the moccasins there.

Connie Robinson and Beatrice Vernon had created a moccasin cottage industry as a "giggle" under licence from Lewiscraft. NeeBees kits were shipped from Canada by the thousands.

"I can make a pair of moccasins in twenty minutes," Vernon told the *Daily Mail*. "They are brought from Canada in three pieces and I have taught thirty women workers how to stitch them together. They do work at home and we hope to reach maximum production of 1,200 pairs a week."

In the *Daily Express*, the 45-year-old said that going into the moccasin business was "the best thing I ever did.

"I got fed up of cooking and cleaning. There was nothing else to do. So I decided to make moccasins because I realized they were becoming very popular."

Part of the appeal of the moccasins appears to have been a (now politically incorrect) romanticizing of the cartoon image of indigenous peoples in the "New World" that had been perpetuated by Hollywood. Ads and packaging played on the popular image of "Indians" in the rugged Canadian wilderness, with handsome models (clearly Caucasian, as was standard practice in advertising back then) wearing war bonnets and feathers, their hands raised in the stereotypical native "how" gesture.

"They are made from . . . bullhide specially brought from the Rockies

Lewiscraft MOCCASIN KITS

THE CLOSEST THING TO BAREFOOT COMFORT

MADE IN CANADA

FROM CANADIAN LEATHER

"SIMPLY LACE AND WEAR"

Full-page product description in the 1964 Lewiscraft catalogue

and prairies of Canada," reads one marketing brochure, "and hand-laced in exactly the same way as the original North American Indian moccasin – the very moccasin that gave the Indian the fleetness of foot for which he was so famous."

The British press were quick to pick up on the "noble warrior" theme. "Mrs. B. goes on the warpath – and sells £5,000 worth of moccasins!" read one 1966 headline about the debut of NeeBees at the Blackpool International

Lewis family Polaroid: "Our moccasins on the sands of the Bahamas"

Slipper Fair. "Moccasins are heap big hit," another said. A photo of a size-50 moccasin created for promotional purposes described it as (you guessed it) "Heap big moccasin."

But if you looked beyond the stereotyping and appropriation of aboriginal culture for commercial purposes that was casually accepted in the 1960s, the NeeBees sales pitch also appealed cleverly to consumers' yearning for authenticity.

"These skins are completely natural," says a brochure. "No artificial dyes at all are used. The colour is tanned into them in the traditional age-old way. The suppleness comes not from processing, but from the extra-thick, heavy quality of the hides. And the markings are Nature's own, like the natural wrinkles of the bull's tremendous shoulders."

Another brochure notes that "no two pairs of NeeBees are alike because no two skins are alike. This history of the bull is written in every pair. The scars, for instance, tell of wounds of barbed wire fences, while the markings are really the huge fat wrinkles of the beasts' tremendous shoulders.

"You will notice, too, that the pairs vary slightly in shade. This is just another proof of their complete authenticity – the result of the lengthy tanning process that each hide has to undergo before it is soft and supple enough for NeeBees."

And, oh, the style and comfort!

> "Fashioned in a style that never dates, never goes out of fashion and can be worn by men, women and children.
>
> "NeeBees are the most comfortable fashion since bare feet. Nee-Bees don't so much hold the feet as enfold them. Thick, supple and soft as kid, the leather moulds itself into a perfect fit, shaping itself round contours and accommodating the broadest foot.
>
> "NeeBees gives the customer two types of footwear for the price of one – an outdoor casual and an indoor slipper. Out-of-doors, they are more comfortable than a casual; indoors they are more hardwearing than a slipper.
>
> "They never date, never change; this type of moccasin has stayed in fashion, unchanged, for over 500 years. How many fashions can boast a record like that?"

And how many companies in the colonies could boast of a simple product, made from leftover raw materials, that took the motherland by storm in a few short years?

Chapter 5
MISS HAMILL

She was one of the most influential and powerful women in Canadian business, in an era when few women had any corporate power or influence.

She began as a part-time stenographer, but was soon running an important division of a company that, by the time she retired, was racking up $6.5 million in annual sales and was loved by women across Canada.

And for much of her forty-one-year career with Lewiscraft, Evelyn Hamill – or, as most everyone knew her, Miss Hamill – carried a melancholy secret.

The story of Lewiscraft would be woefully incomplete without the story of Miss Hamill. And in an odd twist, the only previous attempt to tell the company's story – an informal history commissioned by Lewiscraft leadership in the mid-1990s, but never published – was penned by Miss Hamill herself. Her words from that history (some of them subtly flattering to their uncredited author) punctuate this chapter, in italics.

> *Eldest daughter Ivy now assisted in the office, and, in 1937, she hired Evelyn Hamill as a part-time stenographer. This same Evelyn Hamill became a much-valued employee, spending her entire working career with the company, as well as assisting as a source for this history.*

Born in 1910, Evelyn Sophia Hamill was 27 by the time she signed on to work for Ed. R. Lewis Ltd. in Toronto. Whatever she did before joining the company that eventually became known as Lewiscraft is lost in the mists of time, but it didn't take her long to make an impact on the organization, which had yet to develop its identity as a retailer of craft supplies.

Evelyn Hamill (right), beside Gerry Lewis at company dinner at the King Edward Hotel, 1947

> *It was around 1938 that the Handicraft Division of Ed. R. Lewis was created. . . . A simple, typed product and price list served as a catalogue of available products. Miss Hamill became closely involved in this area of the business, working closely with Fred Lewis, who was responsible for the Handicraft Division. She realized that there was tremendous potential customizing craft kits of particular interest to women. Up to this time, men had been the main target, but now women and children were targeted and became a large part of the clientele for handicraft products.*

By the Second World War, Miss Hamill was leading the handicrafts division, at least partly out of necessity. New company president Gerry Lewis was on the road most of the time meeting with the shoemakers to whom he peddled leather products; some of the company's other senior men were fighting overseas.

"I only know through stories that she was a very integral part of the business and business growth," says Lynda Henry, Gerry's grand-daughter. "She wasn't just sort of part-time. I think she kind of ran the company. Especially around the time of the war."

> In the mid-'40s, the company produced its first little booklet to serve as a catalogue. It was designed and prepared by Evelyn Hamill and Helen Mackay. The artwork was done by Dave Coutie, and the printing was done on an old type duplicating hand machine. It has been quite a step to today's glossy productions! . . .
>
> Through these trying times, the demand on the Handicraft Division continually increased and was ably taken care of by Miss Hamill and her girls. The only male assistance came from Herb Vince and Dave Coutie in the factory. During the war, this small group also took care of the leathercraft needs for occupational therapy requirements of the armed services.

By the early 1950s Lewiscraft was publishing a type-written, four-page booklet every month, mostly written by Miss Hamill in a chatty, down-to-earth voice. Issue No. 1, dated October 1951, had these nuggets:

"Dear Friend:

"With the beginning of the frosty feeling in the air, schools opening, adult education classes forming, comes the always thrilling, vigourous urge for new learning, new skills. None of us is immune! We at Lewiscraft are swept up in this surge of interest in things to do with creative hands, and each season try to have something for you just a little different. . . .

"No doubt most of us have heard and laughed at the expression, 'I can get it for you wholesale.' We try to keep all prices at as low a level as possible so that all may benefit, and honestly feel that a strict adherence to such a policy is in the interests of Better Business throughout the country and is most fair to most people.

"May your creative hands be most successful in this new handicraft season."

"Miss Hamill was sort of Miss Lewiscraft for years before I got there, and after I got there," says Gary Lewis, Gerry's son and the company's third president. "Dad was busy doing the agency business and selling, and Miss Hamill ran the craft side for years.

"(Uncle) Fred was the initiator of the craft business, but he didn't have a business mind at all. Miss Hamill was able to focus and concentrate on it and do all the stuff, the pricing and so forth.

"She definitely was the backbone of the whole company up until I came in."

Everyone called her Miss Hamill, other than Gerry, who called her "Miss Ham." Some employees who worked with her weren't even sure of her first name – one interviewed for this book remembered it as Dorothy (Dorothy Hamill was an American figure skater in the early 1980s).

Miss Hamill was "very reserved and lady-like," remembers Gary's wife, Eleanore. "Very much a lady."

A lady with considerable authority, remarkably so in an era when most women did not hold down paying jobs, and those who did were expected to play traditionally "female" roles such as switchboard operator, stenographer, secretary and sales clerk in the "foundations" department.

By 1944, the handicrafts division had been taken over by a new subsidiary of Ed. R. Lewis: Lewiscraft Art Supplies Ltd. (also called Lewis Craft Art Supplies on some company signs of that era). The company had four officers: president Gerry Lewis, vice-president Fred Lewis, director Harold Pearson . . . and secretary-treasurer Evelyn Hamill.

From that point until her retirement thirty-four years later, Miss Hamill was enmeshed in the company's leadership structure, with primary responsibility for managing the mail-order operation that was Lewiscraft's lifeblood until it began opening retail stores in the 1970s.

She was also someone with a refined understanding of how to play office politics, says Bob Gatfield, Lewiscraft's chief financial officer late in Miss Hamill's career.

"I made the mistake a couple of times early on of doing things she didn't agree with," Gatfield recalls. "Miss Hamill would tell Gerry (who was officially retired but still working every day). Gerry would tell Gary, and Gary would talk to me."

"You really had to wear kid gloves. You couldn't criticize her, couldn't question her decisions, even if they were wrong.

"But she knew the product, knew so many of the old customers, and she was a real customer-first person."

Miss Hamill was "kind of straitlaced and business-like," says Mary Ohorodnyk, who was hired in the early 1950s as an office temp and ended up staying with Lewiscraft for more than forty years. "Very cautious in her manner. She wasn't really someone you could joke around with."

And, of course, she was unmarried – a "spinster" in the lingo of the day. But as a handful of people knew, things might have turned out differently for Miss Hamill.

> In 1941, after a period of ill health, Herb Lewis joined the RCAF and trained as a bomber pilot, graduating at Camp Borden in 1942. He was immediately sent overseas. While in Canada, he would report back to the Handicraft Division and stayed on the payroll, with the then princely salary of $16.00 a week, but the main responsibilities of the Handicraft Division fell on the capable shoulders of Miss Hamill. In appreciation of her role, Herb asked that $2.00 of his pay be allocated to hers for the duration of his absence.
>
> On February 7, 1943, on a bomber raid over a submarine base at Lorient, France, Herb Lewis was shot down and listed as missing in action for six months. Finally, the family was advised that he would not return. He was to have been the future star of the company.

Had Herb returned safely, he and Miss Hamill might very well have married, says Eleanore. "She was in love with Herb."

Instead, with the love of her life killed in the service of his country, Miss Hamill threw herself into her work for the next three decades. In 1978, at

Evelyn (Miss) Hamill, 1975

the age of 68, she retired from Lewiscraft.

In short order, she got married.

"Eleanore came home and said, 'I saw Miss Hamill walking down Yonge Street holding hands with a man!'" says Gary. "I said, 'Bullshit – that can't be true.'"

"Well, lo and behold, I guess it was."

> In 1955, Ruth Shepherd was hired as a crafts counsellor and she assisted in various ways with teaching crafts and demonstrations.... Ruth remained over the years, taking over the position of Mail Order Manager upon the retirement of Evelyn Hamill in 1978 who, at that time, became Mrs. Hartley McKean, residing in Collingwood.

"When we heard that," says Louise Chapdelaine, who worked at Lewiscraft head office starting in 1974, "we were all like, we can't call her Miss Hamill anymore!"

Evelyn Sophia McKean – Miss Hamill, as she will always be known to those who worked with her at Lewiscraft – died in 2007 and was buried in Collingwood, Ontario.

Chapter 6
PRESIDENT IN WAITING

A collision on a football field changed the life of Gary Lewis, and the fortunes of the company his grandfather had founded.

The only child of Gerry and Gladys Lewis, Gary had in various ways been part of the business – which operated as Gerry Lewis Ltd. but was known to Canadians as Lewiscraft – all his life.

As a young boy, he didn't see his father much. Gerry was a workaholic, on the road through the week visiting shoemakers, then working at the company's warehouse on the weekend. Gerry's unwavering devotion to the business in the 1940s and '50s meant that Gary's mother, the former Gladys Coutie, largely looked after rearing the young lad.

"She was so good with Gary because his dad was never home," says Gary's wife, Eleanore. "She'd take him skating and to the show. She was a very integral part in Gary's life.

"She was very gracious, quiet and reserved. Very much a lady; one of the nicest people."

As a teenager, in summers Gary would pack a sandwich (made by his mother) and take the streetcar down to Lewiscraft's warehouse at 8 Bathurst Street, where he did hard manual labour.

"We'd pick up scrap leather from the shoe trade and load it into a freight car. That was physical – great big drums. Very tiring by the end of the day."

Young Gary was not the most attentive student at Malvern Collegiate in Toronto's Beaches district. In fact, he flunked Grade 10. Even so, that same year he was chosen "most popular" student by the school's staff.

No member of the extended Lewis family, including Gerry's brothers and sisters and their offspring, had ever gone past high school. Despite his failure to apply himself at Malvern, Gary managed to get accepted into Ryerson Polytechnic Institute, which had just started offering a diploma

Gary Lewis, early 1960s

in business administration.

Then one of life's little twists of fate came along to change his course. An avid football player, Gary separated his shoulder on the field and had to undergo surgery. Commuting from Scarborough to Ryerson's downtown campus, and unable to play intramural sports, he tried something novel. He worked at his studies.

"My sporting career had come to an abrupt end. And the fact I lived at home instead of being downtown meant I didn't party with the guys all the time. So I came home and just set up in the basement of our house, like an office, with a study schedule.

"I used to always stand last, and then all of a sudden here I am standing first in the class. I won a scholarship every year. It's strange: the harder you work, the luckier you get."

While at Ryerson, Gary joined the Canadian Officer Training Corps, an organization that provided military training to university and college students in case they were ever needed in a conflict. He spent his summers at Camp Borden, north of Toronto, and eventually graduated as a Second Lieutenant in the Royal Canadian Service Corps. (He never had to serve, but during the Cuban Missile Crisis of 1962, "I received a notification saying, be prepared. If they'd gone to war, I would have probably been an instructor or something.")

Even while doing his officer training, Gary never lost his connection to Lewiscraft. In the mid-1950s, the company's most popular product was a do-it-yourself moccasin-stitching kit; Gary sold "cases" of the kits to his fellow trainees in the platoons.

Graduating from Ryerson with honours in 1957, he won the silver medal as the second-best student in the school. A career at Lewiscraft was the natural next step.

"I never had a desire to go anywhere else. It never entered my mind that I would work anywhere else."

But he wasn't going in at the top. Far from it, in fact. His first role as a full-time employee was decidedly unglamourous.

"We would bring plastic lacing from England in big spools, then transfer it onto a small spool. So after three years in business school, my first job was standing in the basement winding plastic lacing onto hundred-yard rolls."

He ended up doing just about every job at Lewiscraft, other than accounting. He loaded and unloaded trucks, stamped out leather products, packaged and mailed craft kits, produced catalogues and handled a variety of office tasks.

If you believe him, he made a hash of many assignments. For a man who grew a fairly small business into a large national brand, Gary is remarkably self-deprecating.

Ask him to describe his career, he replies: "I would just say that I was a retailer and I sold beads and sequins. I might add knitting needles and art supplies and crafts, but basically a beads-and-sequins salesman." (A beads-and-sequins salesman who went on to become chairman of the Retail Council of Canada, mind you.)

Ask him about his early days with Lewiscraft, and he offers a story about filling orders on the leather counter of the company's only store at the time, at 284 King Street West in downtown Toronto.

"A customer would ask for a piece of brown Morocco leather. I'd bring it out and they'd say, 'Brown, not green.' I was colour blind. Every time someone would ask for a colour, I'd have to go back there and ask for help. I could see white on black and black on white, but that was about it."

Colour blindness also affected him years later, as Lewiscraft's president.

"Beads at the time were quite important. I went down to this wholesaler in New York and saw all these nice blue beads. I bought a whole bunch of bags. Well, it turns out they weren't blue. They were purple, and nobody used purple beads. That's when they decided maybe I shouldn't be going on the buying trips. I got fired from being a buyer. It took us years to get rid of those purple beads."

Not only did he get "fired" from his buying position, but the man who would be president also had to give up other tasks.

"We had a printing department for printing instruction sheets. When the fellow who ran it was sick, I used to run the printing press. I didn't know what I was doing and there would be ink all over the place."

There were things he was good at, though, including setting prices on the products the company sold by mail order. He devised a pricing method using a circular slide rule: a type of "mechanical computer" with dials that can be spun around and aligned to make different calculations.

Circular slide rules are used mostly for mathematical functions like trigonometry, and have decreased in use since pocket calculators came to prominence over the past fifty years, but Gary used one as a visual guide to determine profit margins. "A calculator gives you a hard number, but a visual with a slide rule allows you to manipulate the prices better."

He also followed his father's footsteps as a travelling salesman. He would hit the road, visiting hospitals and summer camps, prisons and other institutions that might be in need of craft supplies. Wardens supervising Canada's most notorious criminals, from Kingston Penitentiary to Warkworth Institution, would buy supplies for inmates out of the back of Gary's station wagon.

Working in the Brampton tannery, 1940s

But while spooling lace and spilling ink and hawking Popsicle sticks to institutions, Gary was also gradually learning the finer points of running a business. Working closely with Bruce Pearson, a company adviser and personal mentor, Gary began putting his business education to use.

His first attempt to influence the company's strategic direction came with his review of its tannery operation in Brampton, west of Toronto. Gary's father had bought the tannery, which turned animal hides into leather, in 1946.

Pearson spent a summer as a young man working at the tannery. Asked what he did there, he says: "Took showers most of the time trying to get the stink out!"

"Tanning is a messy, messy business," agrees Gary. "Incredible stink.

"You kill the cow and take the hide off. It has all kinds of flesh and hair on it. The process of de-fleshing and de-hairing is a sloppy, sloppy job. You end up with heavy, thick leather. Not fine leathers like you'd find in wallets or see on a leather coat."

The rough, natural-looking leather produced by the tannery had been used in Lewiscraft's moccasin kits, which sold in the hundreds of thousands across Canada and in the United Kingdom. But by the mid-1960s that product line was waning after a decade as the business's primary revenue source.

Gary was being encouraged by his father to take over running the tannery, but he couldn't see any future for the operation. Moccasins used only a portion of each animal hide, and the market for leather was dwindling because plastics and other synthetic materials were increasingly being used in shoe components. And much of the western hemisphere's tanning was moving to Argentina.

"With everything else stopping, here we are running a tannery just to use the by-product. It's not a good, profitable way to be running a business."

Unable to persuade his father to close the tannery, Gary turned to Pearson, whose own father, Harold, had served as a vice-president of Gerry Lewis Ltd.

"Dad thought Bruce was the cat's meow," Gary says. "Bruce and a friend, Ken May, ran a consulting company. They prepared a formal analysis and presented their findings to Dad.

"They showed it wasn't economically worthwhile to run a tannery just to make by-products. We could get moccasin leather elsewhere rather than run an entire tanning operation. They convinced him he couldn't carry on this way.

"It was more convincing coming from them rather than me. Once he accepted that analysis, he took the advice and sold the tannery."

In 1964, Gary prepared an analysis of Lewiscraft's strengths, weaknesses and opportunities for growth and expansion. The report, hand-written on graph paper, noted that the company had made profit of $57,452 on revenues of $593,923 in 1963 (a 9.7% margin):

> *The craft business offers a terrific potential for the future:*
> *(a) Shorter work weeks – more leisure time*
> *(b) Schools and hospitals introducing craft programs*
> *(c) Growth of craft industry in U.S.A. means more products, better packages, etc.*
> *(d) The increase in population and mixtures of cultures means the introduction of crafts from all over the world*
> *(e) Unofficially about 10% of the population could be interested in crafts, and as a result – potential customers*

Working in the Brampton tannery, 1940s

> *Retail market – this is the area where a tremendous potential exists*
> - *Canada's population: 19,000,000*
> - *% of people possibly interested in crafts: 5% – 950,000*
> - *Estimated existing customers: 300,000*
> - *Potential new customers: 650,000*
>
> *If 10% of potential new customers (65,000) could be achieved per year with an average order of $5, sales increase $325,000 – this would represent an increase of 55% in sales*

Gary burned to achieve such growth. He was determined to build Lewiscraft's annual sales to $1 million. While there would obviously be a corporate benefit from such growth, he had an ulterior motive.

Eager to learn more about business from his peers, he hoped to join the Young Presidents' Organization. The YPO was a global network of individuals – mostly men in the 1960s – who before age 40 were running companies with at least $1 million in sales and 50 employees. (The organization still exists, with higher membership thresholds nowadays.)

Gary's plan, as set out in another handwritten document in the Lewis family archive, had these components:

1. *Sales must increase by an average of 10% per year*
2. *This past year has proven that a wider distribution of catalogues has helped tremendously to educate people as to what Lewiscraft has to offer – this plan must continue and possibly by 1969 we will print 75,000 catalogues*
3. *We must become more flexible in adopting and promoting new products; this can be attained by strengthening our promotion department and making better use of our mailing lists*
4. *An advertising budget should be established, and careful selection of advertising mediums*

Sure enough, company records show that annual revenue broke the $1-million barrier in 1968 after growing seventy-nine per cent over five years.

But that was just the start, as it turned out. Soon, growing the business to $1 million in sales would seem like a quaint relic of the past.

For Gary Lewis had bigger ambitions than just joining the Young Presidents' Organization. He wanted to take his company's goods to where people increasingly were buying – in shopping malls. He wanted to turn Lewiscraft into a retail powerhouse from coast to coast.

Chapter 7
DO IT YOURSELF

Two women were so knowledgeable about knitting, they could make up their own patterns. Another was so dedicated to her needles that she would knit a few stitches in her car while waiting for the light to turn green.

Another turned some pieces of paper, a plastic planter in the shape of a swan and a jar of glue into a national home-decorating craze.

The ladies of Lewiscraft – and the vast majority of store clerks and managers were women, with just a few men sprinkled in – were exactly what the company needed to succeed as it expanded from a mail-order operation into a national retail chain. They were not just dedicated to crafting – they were downright passionate about it.

"Everybody who joined Lewiscraft had to become passionate. You couldn't help it," says Louise Chapdelaine, who held a variety of positions, including oversight of mall outlets. "They were passionate about what we did, what we sold, the craft industry."

Store managers were crafters first and managers second, says Janet Campbell, a senior Lewiscraft executive in the 1970s and '80s. "They loved the product."

And they loved helping customers. If there was one thing Lewiscraft was known for during its heyday, it was the tight bond between regular customers and the employees who often taught them how to make new crafts.

Lewiscraft customers craved the instruction, says Tricia Cadieux, who managed several stores and worked her way up to district manager. "You want people to help because you don't necessarily know what you're doing. To a customer it was like, 'Boy, you guys are really great. You're giving me all this knowledge.'"

A Lewiscraft store was "sort of like a Home Hardware, where the people have the knowledge to pass on to you," says Bruce Pearson, who was an adviser and mentor to company president Gary Lewis.

While some customers stuck to one craft and would come in just to replenish their supply of yarn or glue, others were constantly on the lookout for new things to try. Lewiscraft staff were actively encouraged to learn new crafts that might entice customers looking for something they hadn't made before.

As soon as stock arrived in stores, managers and clerks would crack open the grey plastic tote bins. Each store had a provision in its budget for staff to open packages and see what fresh ideas they could come up with from whatever was inside.

"Everyone would take a crack," says Kim Schell, who managed Lewiscraft's district managers. "We would demonstrate it and have it at the cash register."

Looking back now, the timing seems perfect for Lewiscraft's push into retail.

Originally a wholesale bridge between leather producers and shoemakers, the company had begun selling to individuals during the Great Depression. Resourceful and cash-poor Torontonians would stop by the Lewis warehouse looking for scraps of leather to stitch into wallets or other useful items. Company founder Ed Lewis, who had discovered he could make money by hauling away other companies' scrap leather, was only too happy to sell some of it to ordinary folks.

By the early 1950s, when the concept of the "consumer" was starting to take root in free-market economies, Lewiscraft was selling craft supplies to Canadians through mail order. A monthly company newsletter at the time described crafting as a path to good mental health: "Taking a look over our acquaintances, one quickly notes that the happier and more interesting are they who pursue a hobby and find relaxation from regular work; in so doing, creating a storehouse of interests for retirement years."

The 1960s and early 1970s were a time of enormous social change. The population base shifted from rural Canada to urban centres, which sprawled outwards to suburbs far from the city core and able to support their own shopping centres.

The economy was booming, for the most part. Technical innovations led to the introduction of "modern conveniences" like automatic washers, dryers and dishwashers, creating new leisure time for the women who were typically responsible for household chores.

Women started entering the workforce more than ever before. Many "housewives" took part-time jobs, creating more disposable income for families to spend.

Women also started driving in greater numbers than had been the case through the first half-century of the automobile era. Many families got second cars – perfect for quick and frequent trips to the local mall.

The Summer of Love in 1967 and the rise of the "hippie" movement created a do-it-yourself/express-yourself ethos. Young people made candles, tie-dyed their clothes and got "back to the land" in hand-stitched moccasins.

"Towards the end of the '60s there was an interest in doing stuff with your hands again," says Mary Breen, who worked as a Lewiscraft sales clerk as a teenager, and later founded the Wise Daughters Craft Market in Toronto.

Up until the early 1970s, "doing it yourself was considered very low-end and tacky," says David Demchuk, a lifelong crafter and former author of a blog called Knit Like a Man. "Only poor people made things.

"But then people wanted to get away from a very conformist look. You could go into a craft store, get yarn, make yourself a sweater and be able to say, 'I made this' to your friends. It was a really cool thing."

Gary Lewis's decision to open a chain of retail stores coincided with an era when working with your hands was seen as a good thing, says Shirley Sano, Lewiscraft's art director from 1978 to 1995. "If you did it yourself, you had some input into it. And there was some pride if you did it well.

"To be crafty was a good thing, and if you were crafty and saved money doing it, even better."

Gary Lewis was happy to fill the growing demand for craft supplies. And the opening of more Lewiscraft stores, initially around Toronto and gradually across the country, fuelled the demand.

Agincourt Mall was followed by Sheridan Mall in Toronto's west end, then Albion Mall in the northwest. The first stores outside the Toronto market opened in 1972 in London and Kitchener; the first outside Ontario opened seven years later in Winnipeg.

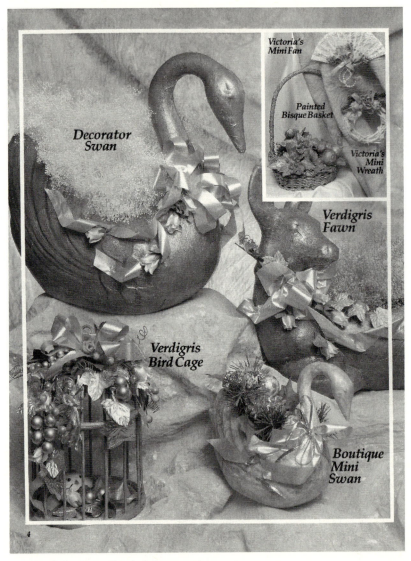

Swans on display in a Lewiscraft Christmas catalogue

As a privately held company operating on fairly tight margins, Lewiscraft lacked the capital required to open stores in many locations at once. Consequently, expansion was slow and measured: two or three new stores most years through the 1970s, slightly greater frequency over the next decade.

"I initially thought the maximum number of stores would be twenty-five," says Gary. "I thought that was very aggressive at the time. Of course when

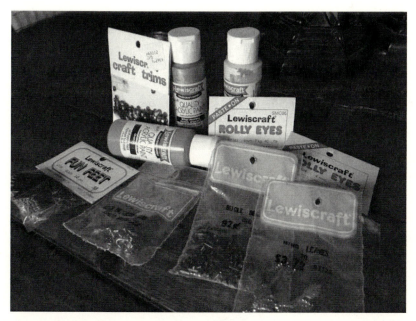

Lewiscraft-branded products (Tricia Cadieux collection)

you get to twenty-five stores you say, 'What the hell, let's keep going.'"

By the time he sold the company in 1995, Lewiscraft had opened seventy-eight stores, in every province except Prince Edward Island (which was considered too small) and Quebec (which was seen as too expensive and complicated because of the French language requirement).

Mall developers like Cadillac Fairview were keen to have Lewiscraft outlets. Even though the stores were small (typically 2,000 square feet, about the size of a large suburban bungalow), they attracted the type of clients desired by malls – mostly women ranging in age from 25 to 55.

The employees reflected the client base not only demographically – most managers and clerks were women in that age range – but in their passion for crafting. Beyond that passion, though, Lewiscraft's employees were also incredibly knowledgeable.

"When I was a store manager I had two ladies who could knit anything – they could make up their own patterns," says Schell. "They knew everything about our yarns. It was incredible how much they knew.

"We had artists who knew the oils and the acrylics. We had younger employees who had done all this stuff at camp, so it was, 'Give me some Popsicle sticks and I'll show you what to do.'"

The craftiness of its employees sometimes led to unforeseen sales trends. A Lewiscraft legend is the story of the swans.

The store in North Bay, Ontario, was suddenly selling far more Podgy, Lewiscraft's store-branded craft glue/sealer, than usual. Head office inquired and was told someone working there had appliquéd some colourful paper to a large plastic swan planter, and put it on display in the store. Now it seemed half the women of North Bay wanted swans and Podgy for their own decoupage projects.

The North Bay manager brought one to a meeting of managers from across the country. The craze went national. "Trailer loads of swans coming in," says Mackie. "It was nuts."

"My God, we couldn't get them in fast enough," adds Cadieux. "We'd be ordering them by the hundreds. Everybody was doing the Podgy swans."

Over the course of two or three years, "these plastic swans sold a gazillion jars of Podgy," says Gord Lewis, who worked as a vice-president before and after his father sold the company. "The amount of revenue directly related to this one single project was phenomenal."

Lewiscraft regularly ran in-store classes to teach customers new crafts. Some classes were "make-and-takes," where attendees would go home with a finished product.

If classes were done at the front of the store, "you'd be demonstrating to the mall," says Mark Mattin, a clerk in several Toronto stores during the 1970s.

"It was a fantastic place to work because you could say, 'I really want to try enamel work,' and your manager would say, 'Well, go and make something.'"

While the vast majority of Lewiscraft employees were middle-aged women, Mattin was a young man. He applied for a job at the Lewiscraft store in Golden Mile Shopping Centre a few weeks before it opened in 1974. For many years Golden Mile, in the Toronto suburb of Scarborough, was Lewiscraft's largest store (about 6,000 square feet); Mattin was one of Lewiscraft's youngest employees (17) and undoubtedly its tallest (six-foot-seven).

A crafter his whole life, he was working full-time at the post office to help his family make ends meet when he took on a second time job at Lewiscraft.

"When I had my interview I was able to say, 'I crochet, I knit, I macramé,

Young Gord Lewis on duty at the warehouse, 1980s

I paint, I sculpt, I make costumes.' I did everything. I was hired on the spot as a sales clerk – which meant sales clerk, craftsperson, workshop leader, demonstrator and cashier.

"I considered it to be challenging gender roles. Remember, 1975 was the very first International Woman's Year, and there I was in the middle of the store."

Mattin was frequently called upon to teach classes.

"You'd come into work and they'd say, 'Tonight you're giving a crocheting class.' We'd have 17 ladies signed up. They're like, 'We're here for the workshop,' and I'm like, 'Take a seat, take off your coat.'

"I'd be fussing and they'd think, Madame's going to come in and teach us. And all of a sudden I'd say, 'Now, go and pick up your . . .' and they'd be stunned.

"It was very interesting to see people's faces when they realized that I was going to teach them how to knit a pair of slippers. They'd ask me, 'When did you learn to knit?' and I would say, 'I've done it my entire life.'"

Gord Lewis was not just an executive – he, too, learned how to knit. He describes visiting a store and serving a customer, an older woman. He asked

A typical Lewiscraft mall store, this one in Oshawa

if she knew how to "carry colours" – a knitting technique where different balls of yarn can be used simultaneously. She didn't. So Gord immediately pulled out two chairs, set them up in the middle of the store, and proceeded to give the woman a knitting tutorial.

"I said, 'Do you want me to show you?' I showed her how to do it. I could see the store manager behind the counter watching with astonishment."

There was a clear focus on making sure staff knew the product and had tried it, says Cadieux. "Hands on so they could serve the customer better. It was, 'Did you see what we got in last week?' So you get the customer service and the opportunity to increase your sale."

It wasn't just about serving customers and upselling, though. Lewiscraft employees simply loved making crafts. Lynda Henry, Gary Lewis's daughter who worked as a product buyer, recalls how evident this was at the annual meetings of store managers.

"We would have product knowledge sessions where they would actually do a craft. You'd never see a manager rolling their eyes and going, 'Oh, crap, I can't believe we have to do this.' They were all into it – they loved it. Even the hokiest things – I mean, we had some hokey crafts."

Love of crafting compensated for the fact that – as is typically the case in retail sales – staff didn't make much money. "They were totally dedicated and they weren't highly paid," admits Gary.

Staff did get discounts on merchandise, though – sometimes as much as 40 per cent off the retail price.

"Most of us spent our paycheques at Lewiscraft," says Mona Kleperis, who worked as an artist at head office.

"If you are a crafter and you work in Lewiscraft, guess where a lot of your pay goes?" adds Mary Gillis, who worked as an assistant store manager. "All the new stuff coming in – you've got to have that."

Gord Lewis notes that when he left the company in 1996, a store manager was making about $28,000 a year. "That always bothered me. You couldn't appropriately reward the ones that were outstanding because the stores just didn't make enough money to do it.

"The good ones treated it like it was their own store."

Chapter 8
THE BALLS TO BE GOOD

They had to get the olives. That was a given.

A few senior staff members from Lewiscraft's head office would fly out to set up a new store in a shopping centre somewhere in Canada.

Kim Schell, who was not only manager of Lewiscraft's store supervisors but also the undisputed expert at new-store setup, would be part of the head-office delegation. So would Alec Coutie, a senior executive who also happened to be a first cousin of Gary Lewis, the company's owner.

Alec and Kim would pick up a car at the airport, then head to the nearest liquor store. There were long, gruelling days ahead, after all, and the setup crew would need to kick back at night.

Another stop also had to be made. The grocery store. To pick up a jar of olives.

At the end of the day, the setup crew would convene in someone's hotel room. The bar would open and Alec would start pouring drinks – and helping himself to olives.

"We usually didn't have a spoon, so Alec would just stick his hand in the jar and pull them out," Schell says with a fond smile. "Those were really, really fun times."

As Lewiscraft expanded across the country, from its first mall store in 1969 to its seventy-eighth twenty-five years later, a small group of employees handled most store setups. Coutie and Schell might be joined by chief buyer Mary Mackie, chief operating officer Janet Campbell, art director Shirley Sano, district manager Louise Chapdelaine, sometimes Gary Lewis himself and, in later years, Gary's son, Gord.

They schlepped crates of products in from trucks, arranged colourful displays at the ends of each aisle and the store front, and trained the store's

Alec Coutie, 1975

staff on how everything worked.

A big part of the job in the early years of the stores was stapling burlap to pegboards. The walls were covered in burlap, with merchandise hung on hooks pressed into it.

"The burlap was the grossest job in the world," remembers Mackie. "Itchy, itchy, itchy. We'd hand-staple the stuff up there and try to get it nice and squared off and folded over the edges. Then you'd take those stupid peg hooks and have to ram them through the burlap."

By the end of a day of stapling and ramming, "your fingers were raw," says Schell.

The burlap was a dust magnet, and the pegboards it was stapled to may have been highly flammable. Yet when the company later switched to "slat walls" – with grooves embedded to hold display pegs – "everybody was up in arms," says Chapdelaine. "Managers were saying we looked like a hardware store. That decision wasn't popular at first, but I think everybody realized

Display plans were drawn in ink on graph paper by Mona Jeige and sent to stores

after a while that it was a smart move. The burlap held so much dust."

Schell opened so many stores over two decades that she eventually was able to do it with a much smaller crew, using detailed illustrations – known as plan-o-grams – she'd prepared in advance.

"They would send the stores a prototype display," says Mark Mattin, who worked as a clerk in several Toronto-area stores. "You would set the display up based on their prototype. Someone would have sketched it. And of course the sketch itself was a work of art."

But even with good systems, problems occurred from time to time. Schell remembers one near-disaster at Metrotown shopping centre in Burnaby, British Columbia.

"It was the opening of the entire mall. We walked into the store and there was nothing done. Absolutely nothing. There was supposed to be slat wall installed by the contractor, and instead it was concrete block. I called Alec and I was almost crying.

"Alec called the contractor's office and said, 'You get him there right now.' I remember Alec saying to me, 'I'll have his balls for bookends.'"

Finishing construction took several days, leaving little time to set up displays and stock shelves.

"We couldn't start the actual setup until 5 o'clock the night before opening day. We bought chips and pop, chocolate milk and chocolate bars and said, it's going to be an all-nighter. We finished about 9 a.m.

"The computers were up and running, we had the cash ready to go, and right before we were to open the doors, the ceiling started leaking. It was like a river coming down, so we had garbage cans collecting the water. But we got it open. That was our closest shave."

For stores near Toronto, the company president would often be part of the setup crew – doing the most menial labour. "Gary would be there sweeping and taking out garbage," says Mackie. "Cutting up boxes."

Lynda Henry, Gary's daughter, remembers him impressing a local labourer who had been brought in to help with setup. "He came up to my dad and said, 'You are a really good worker. If you ever need a job...' My dad said, 'Um, thanks!'"

Sweeping up at openings wasn't the only time Gary Lewis went to Lewiscraft's stores. He made a point of visiting each outlet about once a year. These were not "secret shopper" ambushes – he let managers know he was coming, figuring that if the store was not ship-shape for the president's visit, there must really be a problem.

Staff were so keen to meet the boss – and so chuffed that there really was a Lewis behind the Lewiscraft brand – that clerks scheduled for a day off would often go into the store just to see him.

Once there, Gary chatted with staff (often drawing on his own notes from past visits to inquire about family members). He asked and answered questions – and smiled constantly.

"Gary always had time to listen to people," says Mackie. "'Maybe that's something we can look into.' That was a big thing with him."

He didn't issue orders, adds Mattin. Just the opposite, in fact. "He's not telling you, he's asking you. He'd want to know what's going on and he'd approve it, but he wouldn't say no, no, no."

Gary had a personality "that brought out the best in people," says Tricia Cadieux, who held a variety of senior roles with Lewiscraft. "He treated people, especially at head office, like a family."

And he made friends with just about everyone he came in contact with. For a while he served as chairman of the wholesale division of the Hobby Association of America.

"He knew everybody in the craft industry," says Mackie. "At trade shows, you used to hate having Gary come with you because you'd be walking down the aisle and it was, 'Gare! Gare! Gare! How ya doin'? How ya doin'?' He'd stop to chat, and twenty-five minutes later you're still standing there."

Gary himself says he always made a concerted effort not to put on airs

Gord Lewis (foreground) and Bob Gatfield setting up a new store

or view himself as superior to others – a trait he picked up from his father, Gerry Lewis. "When I talk to anybody, I'm on the same level as them. The kids call me Fred Friendly."

That philosophy coursed through Lewiscraft. "I can't think of anybody who had airs," says Lynda, who worked for several years in senior roles. "If somebody thought they were better than anybody else, they weren't there very long."

"The way people interacted with each other – with respect and honesty and integrity – was expected at head office and flowed down from there," adds son Gord Lewis, who also held senior positions.

Gary believed in hiring good people, and letting them do their jobs.

"A lot of entrepreneurs and company presidents are afraid to hire better than themselves," says Lynda. "That fear wasn't there for him. He hired the smartest people he could afford, and we had a lot of really smart people that worked there."

Janet Campbell, 1985

One of the smartest was Janet Campbell. Hired as merchandise manager in the mid-1970s, she became one of the company's most powerful executives as chief operating officer.

If anything, she had even greater ambitions for Lewiscraft than Gary Lewis. Along with chief financial officer Bob Gatfield (whom Campbell married late in life), she brought rigorous business discipline to the company.

"She was the driving force behind Lewiscraft," says Mackie, who worked under Campbell as chief buyer. "She would always push us to get to the next level.

"Janet had the balls to say we're going to be good."

Led by Campbell and Gatfield, Lewiscraft was an early adopter of modern retail technology. It was one of the first companies in Canada to use the Universal Product Code (the bar code found on products) – a valuable tool in a business that typically stocked 12,000 separate items in its warehouse.

"It was tough to manage inventory in the early days," says Chapdelaine. "For example, little squares of felt came in like twenty-five or thirty-six colours. We had someone go in the warehouse every day with a pad of paper and count how many we had. The new systems brought in automatic replenishment for the stores. They didn't have to order anymore because it was automated."

"We were leading edge in many ways," Campbell says. "Point of sale data capture: we had it before Eaton's. Computerized inventory management. And computerized connection with suppliers.

"I remember when we first got a fax machine and could actually send orders to the Orient without using the mail. That was quite something."

By the 1980s the stores had hand-held devices to enter sales figures, employee hours and other financial information. Using an acoustic coupler to connect to a central computer in the pre-Internet days, stores could upload their data each week to head office.

Campbell was intensely focused on maximizing profit – not always easy in a business driven by very small individual sales, and with generous customer service.

"We had to have staff who, if you had a problem, could show you how to knit, do this and that," says Gary. "You'd walk out after buying five dollars' worth of stuff. Meanwhile it had cost us ten dollars to pay the employee to teach you. But that was really what separated us from a lot of other stores, the fact that we could look after you."

Lewiscraft brought in $35 million in revenue at its peak in 1994. The average sale at that point was about eight dollars – which means there were a hell of a lot of transactions.

"That used to drive Janet nuts," says art director Shirley Sano, who reported to Campbell. "Towards the end, the buyers and I were given the sales printouts. Janet would say, 'Look at this – $3.02.'"

Products were typically marked up 100 per cent over cost. But labour, occupancy and operating costs were, as a percentage of revenue, higher than most other retailers'.

The infamous naked Santa (Eileen Woods crochet work)

"You're talking about a bag of beads selling for $1.29," says Gord Lewis. "Somebody's got to pick that out of the warehouse, put it in a bin, put it on a truck, drive the truck to the store, take it off the truck and put it on the wall."

Yarn generated good cash flow because a customer knitting a heavy sweater might need ten balls of wool. "So it was a thirty-dollar sale as opposed to beads and some rolly eyes, which was a five-dollar sale," says Mackie.

The business was incredibly seasonal, pulling in between sixty and seventy-five per cent of annual revenue in the fall. "Christmas was huge," says Gary. Then came January, February and March. "You starved to death."

While Christmas was when Lewiscraft made most of its money, one year Campbell made one of her few big mistakes on a Yule-related purchase. She bought a truckload of naked Santa Claus dolls that didn't sell.

"All they had on were little black boots," says Chapdelaine. "She thought they were the best thing because people could knit or make little clothes and dress them up.

"Well, these naked Santas hung around for years. At one Christmas party she had at her house, she wrapped them all up and gave each one of us a naked Santa for Christmas.

"I still have mine. I bring him out every Christmas."

Chapter 9

CANADA'S CRAFT CATALOGUE

Lewiscraft was built on customers exercising creative impulses to make pretty things. Yet the engine that drove the business in the 1960s – the Lewiscraft catalogue – was put together for a few years by a guy who had no creative juices flowing.

"I'm colour blind and not the least bit crafty, yet it was my job to make the damn catalogue," says Gary, who back then was on his way to becoming president of Lewiscraft.

"The catalogues I did were just straight pictures with a bit of copy. No imagination and no creativity."

He would head down to the basement of Lewiscraft's office and warehouse on King Street West in Toronto, Polaroid camera in hand.

"Put the product on the stand, snap a picture of it, then paste it in. No creativity. It was like, we're selling a cup, so here's a picture of a cup.

"I got fired from that job. I was delighted to get out of it because it wasn't my strength. The later catalogues had some artistic flair, mine were pretty basic."

Artistic flair arrived in the late 1970s with the hiring of Shirley Sano as Lewiscraft's art director.

Sano established the "look and feel" of Lewiscraft in catalogues and store displays for close to two decades as the company became an arts and crafts supplier beloved by tens of thousands of Canadians. During Lewiscraft's aggressive growth spurt of the 1980s, her words and pictures helped countless customers learn about the craft products the company sold.

"The catalogues before I arrived were a bit hokey," Sano says. "I tried to make the presentation a little better."

Presentation mattered to Lewiscraft in the 1970s and '80s. Even while the company was opening a handful of new stores each year, it continued mailing out tens of thousands of catalogues: 132 pages (or more) of ideas and products for dedicated crafters to pore over.

Lewiscraft was a magical world of craft supplies available almost nowhere else, and most of them could be ordered from the catalogue. If it lacked the mythic status of the Eaton's catalogue (not to mention the heft – no boy ever strapped Lewiscraft catalogues to his shins as makeshift goalie pads), it was nonetheless a slice of Canadiana representative of a bygone era.

Lewiscraft's direct sales had begun in the mid-1940s with the production of the first catalogue – actually a small booklet – designed in part by Evelyn Hamill, who would manage the mail-order business for most of the next three decades. It was printed on a hand-duplicating machine at first, and later on a printing device called a Gestetner, which used stencils on rotating drums to crank out copies of typed documents.

The first edition of the "Lewiscraft Newsletter" was produced and circulated in October of 1951. Printed on eleven-by-seventeen-inch cardstock, it consisted of two chatty, typewritten pages of product suggestions signed by Miss Hamill, ads for bisque figurines and "pre-sketched" painting kits, and a page of craft hints credited to "Ray Potter, speaking for Lewiscraft."

Miss Hamill's photograph appeared in the newsletter's logo in February of 1952, and two years later the first full-sized catalogue was produced: fifty-two pages of craft and hobby materials to suit every taste. The cardboard cover listed fourteen activities for the do-it-yourselfer, including leathercraft, Dresden craft, shellcraft, basketry, metal tooling, glove making and clay modelling. "For every hobbyist! For every craftsman! A complete handicraft catalogue offering quality merchandise at prices that please!"

The first seventeen pages of the catalogue were devoted to leathercraft products: leather itself, moccasins, adhesives, dyes, cleaners, tools, stamps, lacing, buckles, clasps, accessories and books. There was also a handy guide to the different varieties of leather, noting the differences between "kip" (leather from a half-grown cow or steer), "belly" (softer leather from the flank, "recommended for beginners and classrooms") and "skiver" ("the top grain from sheepskin leather... recommended only for lining billfolds, belts, etc.").

The centrespread extolled the virtues of a craft that disappeared altogether from later editions: shellcraft. Eighty-seven varieties of seashells were

available at prices ranging from seven cents each to $6.25 a pint.

The 1954 catalogue (identified as "No. 54" rather than by its date) also began what would become a Lewiscraft tradition: crazily named products, in this case Fluf-E-Kote. It was a substance used for flocking (the process of depositing many small fibre particles, called flock, onto a surface):

"Paint the surface with an adhesive, then blow or dust on Fluf-E-Kote, let dry, then shake lightly to eliminate excess flock that has not adhered to the surface. A deep, even coat results, giving you a rich velvet covering." Fluf-E-Kote came with a few accessories including a cardboard "gun" applicator.

Product ordering instructions were located on the inside back cover: "Use postal, express or money orders. If you must use cash, please register your letter as we cannot accept responsibility for loss of cash sent by mail. If forwarding cheque from outside Toronto, please add 25 cents to cover the cost of Bank Exchange." Cash on Delivery orders were also accepted: "C.O.D. orders should total $2.00 or more; please remit (payment) with order for smaller amounts."

Continuing a theme first articulated in Miss Hamill's early-1950s newsletters, the 1957 catalogue had a full page pitched to a target demographic: retirees. "Leisure hours (that) senior citizens seem to have such an abundance of – certainly not of their own choosing – can be turned into hours of productive and satisfying accomplishments through a handicraft project

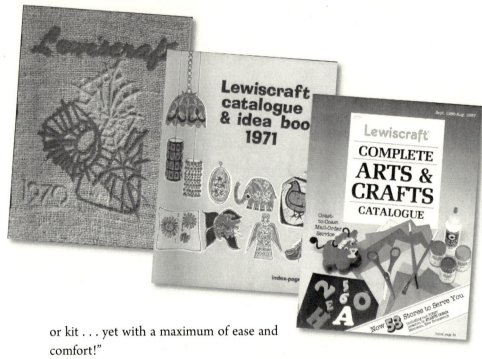

or kit . . . yet with a maximum of ease and comfort!"

By 1963, the fiftieth anniversary of the company started by Ed Lewis, the catalogue (credited as "No. 50") was full of crafts reflective of an era when women had more leisure time and suburbs were bursting with kids born during the Baby Boom. Popsicle sticks (later rebranded as "craft sticks") and pipe cleaners (grandly called "chenille stems") were inexpensive products that could be used in countless crafts.

Leather was still dominant at twenty-four pages, but newer featured products included raffene (synthetic raffia), mosaic kits, paint-by-numbers art, do-it-yourself lampshades, corkcraft and the first appearance of Maple-Rok: "The most fascinating carving medium of our century! Our geologists call it diatomite of an extraordinary kind, stained properly, compressed properly and bonded to give just the right consistency, hardness and texture for perfect carving." (Who knew Lewiscraft had geologists?)

"It's a snapshot into an era," says David Demchuk, who grew up in a Winnipeg home that regularly received supplies ordered from the catalogue.

Paging through old catalogues is like stepping back in time for Demchuk: "Here's our faux hippie person. Macaroni craft. Styrofoam – you would be decorating your home in Styrofoam.

"We made a million things out of Popsicle sticks and clothes pegs.

This stuff was incredibly critical to us. We learned so much just from the catalogue."

Lewiscraft catalogues were full of distinctive, sometimes bizarre, product names and blurbs. Here are a few samples of the "lingo of Lewiscraft":

Podgy: Lewiscraft's very own formula. Podgy is a glue, glaze and sealer – all in one! Every home should have a jar of Podgy. It is so economical you will never want to be without it. NOTE: Do not order Podgy or Mod Podge in winter months. It's not workable if frozen.

Dip-it: A fascinating new craft material for making graceful floral arrangements, mobiles, jewelry, etc. Ten Canadian-made ounces of liquid plastic. But more than that, it is the pathway to a word of lights, glass-like decorations, free-form fantastical shapes, flowers, mobiles, jewelry and more – much more.

Decal-it: Create authentic-looking oil paintings without using a single drop of paint!

Crackle-it: A fast shrinking glaze that is used over Decal-it to create "age" cracks. Makes a 16th-century print look like an authentic painting!

Rub 'n' Buff: Take an ordinary, every-day, rather dull figure. Dab at it with this stuff. Buff it . . . and poof! The magical genie that is you has transformed it into a weathered antique, spoils from the tomb of King Tut, a living statue, a colourful plaque. Apply to anything (with the exception of front teeth) for beautiful highlights.

Crystlettes: Transparent plastic crystals you "bake" in your oven!

Phentex: A modern new knitting yarn of 100% "Celaspun." Phentex's colours never fade or deteriorate and can be machine washed under normal conditions.

Boot-moc: Authentically styled after the famous Indian "Squaw Boot," featuring a fringed cuff and a true moccasin toe piece.

The cyclical, faddish nature of crafting is readily apparent by browsing through catalogues from the Lewis family archives.

Make-your-own moccasin kits, Lewiscraft's first mass-marketed product, were up front and sometimes even shown in colour in the early 1960s. Lewiscraft also offered "Indiancraft" products, including a "beginner's war

"Creepy" doll heads from a Lewiscraft catalogue

bonnet kit," a "Special Chief headdress kit" and an assortment of tomahawks, peace pipes, rattles, feather armbands, bear claws and eagle feathers.

The moccasin kits were buried on page 107 by 1969 (the same year Lewiscraft began accepting payment by Chargex, the forerunner of today's Visa credit card). Moccasins were down to a postage-stamp-sized ad in 1981, and gone altogether by 1987.

Macramé – heavy cord woven with beads to make hanging planters and the like – made its first appearance in 1973; by 1976 it took up the first six pages of the catalogue.

"The biggest single craft ever was macramé," says Gary Lewis. "It was huge for a couple of years. We were bringing in jute and beads from the Orient by the carload."

Lamp-making was featured in the early 1970s. Rug hooking and a related hobby called "latch craft" were the hot items a decade later. The catalogue depicted three-dimensional figures named Eminence Owl and Who Owl, with ceramic eyes and beaks included: "Perch these on your wall."

"Those ugly owls," says Mary Mackie, Lewiscraft's head buyer. "We were going, 'Oh my God, who wants to put this in their house?' It was painful. Some of it we would just laugh about – but we knew they would sell well. You just had to get over it."

Then there were the plastic heads. The customer was supposed to make a doll and then attach one of the heads. But more than a few Canadians were totally creeped out by catalogue pictures of those heads.

"Terrifying dolls which I can't even look at," says Demchuk. "Those clowns haunted my childhood."

Lynda Henry, a member of the Lewis family who for a time made the rounds of morning TV shows as "Lynda Lewis of Lewiscraft," recalls going on a CBC-TV program hosted by Ralph Benmergui.

"He said to me, 'So what is it with those half doll faces – those are really creepy.' I said to him with a most serious face, 'Actually, those are one of our biggest sellers.' He said, 'Really?' I said, 'No.'

"He wasn't impressed. His crew thought it was hilarious but he didn't like that. But they are creepy."

Canada's Craft Catalogue

Mary Breen, who worked as a clerk at Sherway Gardens in Toronto and Square One in Mississauga, "took a particularly weird elf head, stuck it on a bottle of glue, made a little cartoon bubble reading, 'Need glue?' and put it by the cash."

Gary Lewis, making one of his periodic store visits, noticed it and said, "I need to send a memo to all the stores: put an elf head on the glue with a bubble that says, 'Need glue?' He was really pleased with me. And really I was just goofing around with a scary elf head."

⌒

The person who approved the pictures and copy of those creepy doll heads was Shirley Sano. Becoming Lewiscraft's art director in 1978 was the culmination of a dream she'd had from the time she was a young girl.

Born in Vancouver during the Second World War, when many citizens of Japanese descent were placed in internment camps, Sano was separated from her parents because of the tensions caused by war in the Pacific. She was

Beads and Sequins: The Lewiscraft Story

THE ONE-HOUR PLANT HANGER

#74310   25¢

A SPECIALLY DESIGNED SIMPLE PLANT HANGER... THAT ANYONE CAN MAKE IN ONE HOUR

IT'S INEXPENSIVE! IT'S EASY! IT'S FUN! MAKE ONE FOR YOURSELF & ONE FOR A FRIEND

MATERIALS NEEDED:
29.3 m, 5 ply jute
16 - 16mm beads
Macrame board
T pins

NOTE: THE FINISHED LENGTH OF THE HANGER IS 112 cm
To shorten the hanger by 15 cm omit step 8. The number of beads required to make the shorter hanger will be 8 (per hanger). The overhand knot in step 9 can then be adjusted to the proper length.

INSTRUCTIONS

1. Cut 16 cords 1.8 m long.

2. Tie all the cords together with an overhand knot.

3. Divide 16 cords into 4 groups of 4 cords. Make 1 square knot with each group 2.5cm away from the overhand knot.

4. Join 2 cords from 1 square knot and 2 cords from the adjacent square knot, all the way around. You now have 4 new groups of 4 cords each.

5. Now, working with these new groups, make a square knot 5cm away from the previous knot. Take the 2 centre cords and make an overhand knot. Now make another square knot.

6. Separate the cords again as in step 4. Leave 10cm & tie a square knot, an overhand knot, then a square knot with each group.

7. Repeat separation. Leave 13cm space, tie 2 square knots. Thread 1 bead on the 2 centre cords. With these 2 cords, make an overhand knot. Thread another bead on the same cords. Now, make another 2 square knots.

8. Leave 11.4 cm; using the same 4 cords, tie 1 square knot, then thread a bead on the 2 centre cords. Tie an overhand knot, then thread a bead on the 2 centre cords and tie a square knot.

9. To finish off your hanging planter, take all the ends and tie an overhand knot to the desired length.

10. To make the fringe, unravel the 5 plys of each strand of jute, both at the bottom and top of the plant hanger.

Lewiscraft
Toronto • Canada • M1S 3S2

sent to London, Ontario, at the age of four, to be raised by an older couple. They happened to be the grandparents of a young lad named David Suzuki, who grew up to become a well-known environmentalist and broadcaster.

Shirley and her sister shared a bedroom in the Suzuki residence. "There was paper and crayons beside the bunk beds and I drew all over every square inch of paper. They said, 'You're an artist.'"

In high school, she had good grades but no desire to pursue higher

Canada's Craft Catalogue

education. "I announced to Grandma that I wanted to be an artist. I wanted to pursue my dream."

Sano was working as a commercial artist when she saw a newspaper ad for the job of art director at Lewiscraft. She was hired by Janet Campbell, Lewiscraft's manager of merchandising.

While Campbell pitched in on the writing from time to time, most of the copy that accompanied sketches or photos of products came from the pen of Sano, who also decided where items would be placed in the book. She and assistant Mona Jeige (who later married and changed her surname to Kleperis), pasted everything onto production sheets.

Kleperis, who developed enormous respect for Sano as an artist and a leader, says her boss always delivered what was required. "You could give Shirley a project in the morning and she'd say, 'I don't have time to do this.' The next day it was done. And it was not just done, it was done."

Sano abhorred wasting money. Kleperis remembers Sano noticing an X-ACTO knife blade in the garbage can and asking why it had been discarded.

"I said, 'The blade's dull.' If you're cutting and pasting a lot, they get dull.

She pulled out this stone and started sharpening the blade. I thought, it's worth ten cents, I don't have the time to sharpen something that is worth ten cents."

⁂

Even while Lewiscraft was growing its retail presence with two or three new stores each year during the 1970s, catalogue distribution rose. The company printed nearly 40,000 catalogues in 1971, more than double that total three years later. By 1991, though, circulation was below 30,000.

Campbell and Gary agreed it was time to kill the catalogue in early 1994.

"The time was nigh," Campbell says. "It was really becoming a bit of a noose around the neck, quite frankly. We let it die its own little death as the stores opened. It just dwindled because we were coast to coast, really, at that point."

Campbell's internal memo announcing its demise described the catalogue as "the foundation upon which the stores were built and the chain expanded."

The death of the Lewiscraft catalogue occurred around the same time as Gerry Lewis, Gary's father, finally stopped going to work. Although he had officially retired as company president in 1969, Gerry continued going into the office for 25 years while his son ran the show.

Gerry's vision of Lewiscraft had always been built around the mail-order business and the catalogue.

Even into his 90s, he had final sign-off authority on the book. If there was a typographical error, or last year's price on an item hadn't been updated, inevitably it would be discovered by the elder Lewis.

"He was like a mongoose," says Bob Gatfield, who was chief financial officer. "So focused on that.

"I guess that was a carry-forward from his day. He was a cataloguer, not a retailer."

Chapter 10
DROPPING A STITCH OR TWO

The final three decades of the Lewis family's stewardship of Lewiscraft – from the mid-1960s growth of the mail-order business to the opening of retail stores from coast to coast – could only be described as a roaring success. But not everything the business tried worked out as planned.

Despite Lewiscraft's strong growth trajectory in the 1970s and '80s, Gary Lewis never seriously considered expanding into the United States. That market was too large and had too much competition – and as a family-owned business that did not rely on outside capital, Lewiscraft took a slow-but-steady approach to expansion across Canada, opening only a few new stores each year.

But the Lewiscraft banner did fly briefly outside Canada. If you visited Leeds, England, in the early 1970s, you might have discovered a Lewiscraft store. It was one of two branches of the chain in England – with the same name, logo and signage, and many of the same products that could be purchased at Westmount Mall in London, Bonnie Doon Shopping Centre in Edmonton or any other Canadian Lewiscraft outlet.

Gary, the final family member to own the company, opened the UK stores in partnership with a Brit named Jack Aldous, who was himself a third-generation member of a crafting clan. In fact, the parallels to Lewiscraft are uncanny.

Aldous was the grandson of Fred Aldous, who in the late nineteenth century had started a business selling cane and willow to basket weavers. Fred's son, known as "Fred the Second," steered the business towards handicrafts after the First World War, and found a steady clientele in schools, women's institutes and local guilds. A century later, craft shops that look remarkably similar to Lewiscraft stores still operate under the Fred Aldous banner in

Manchester and Leeds.

Jack Aldous, son of Fred the Second, had struck out on his own in 1960, purchasing a company called Atlas Handicrafts. Atlas became the UK distributor for Lewiscraft's wildly popular moccasin kits, and Lewiscraft in turn sold Atlas's crafting guides.

Gary flew overseas to help Aldous merchandise the moccasin kits. "Jack and I got talking, over a bottle of gin, about the craft business in England, and decided, why not give it a try? Set up a Lewiscraft store."

They opened an outlet in Preston, Lancashire, followed by the one in Leeds, West Yorkshire.

"We duplicated as much as we could from the Canadian example," Gary says. However, the notion proved simpler in concept than execution. Initially stock was shipped over from Canada, but that wasn't economical, and sourcing products from Europe proved to be too challenging.

"We thought it would be great to open stores throughout England, but three or four years after we opened the second store we realized it wasn't going anywhere and we had to close them down," Gary says. "It was not what you'd call a success story – a short-lived experiment. I can't remember if we actually lost money, but in any case it was not a profitable venture."

Another venture Gary would like to forget was a short-lived diversification effort. During a period in the 1980s when knitting was driving a large portion of Lewiscraft's revenues, he decided to open stores specializing in yarn, under a different banner. Lynda's Yarns was born.

As one of Canada's largest retailers of wool, Gary knew Jock White, the president of Patons & Baldwins, one of the biggest yarn suppliers. After talking to White about the seemingly unstoppable growth of knitting, "I got the idea that maybe we should have a chain of knitting stores. Knitting was huge at the time."

Lynda's Yarns was aimed at "higher-end knitters doing sophisticated sweaters," says Mary Mackie, who worked as head buyer for Lewiscraft.

The company opened five or six small Lynda's Yarns outlets in shopping centres – just as knitting fell off in popularity among crafters. "The yarn business just nose-dived," Gary says ruefully "Talk about bad timing. We just had to fold our tent and get out. Take your licks and move on.

"We try to forget that."

The stores were named after Gary and Eleanore Lewis's eldest daughter, who at the time was rising through the ranks of Lewiscraft. Now Lynda Henry, she describes the spinoff with a bemused smile as "a whopping flop that I had nothing to do with."

The worst day in the history of Lewiscraft – perhaps the worst day in the life of its president, Gary Lewis – was the day he learned one of his trusted lieutenants had been stealing money from the company. And not just petty cash. When the full extent of the embezzlement was uncovered, half a million dollars had been lost.

Like most retail businesses, Lewiscraft had to deal on occasion with dishonest staff. With craft supplies selling for small amounts, it would have been easy for clerks or even managers to pocket the odd ten-dollar bill rather than put it into the cash register. While no enterprise likes losing even a dime, a slight erosion of revenue to occasional employee theft isn't unexpected and can be factored into financial planning.

But this wasn't a small, easy-to-dismiss problem. Sales were good and yet the organization was falling short on cash flow, with no obvious explanation.

Gary spent nights tossing and turning in bed, remembers his wife, Eleanore. "Where's the money?" he would say. "I don't know why we're not making money."

Then one day the company's auditor came in and said, "We've got a problem. There's a cheque for $50,000 that's not right."

"A cheque for $50,000?" replied an incredulous Gary.

That was just a hint of the problem. The auditor uncovered that an accountant – who not only worked in the office but also played on the company's recreational softball team – had embezzled more than $500,000. He had shown up at work with new cars, explaining to trusting colleagues that he'd won a lottery or received an inheritance.

"We didn't know it but we had been running five travel agencies," says Gary. "He was running them using our money."

Discovering the money had been siphoned was "a devastating day," says Bob Gatfield, the chief financial officer who managed the accountant. Gatfield, who felt responsible, offered to resign; Gary, loyal to his executive team, refused to accept.

Lewiscraft called in the police fraud squad. The accountant ended up going to jail.

This was a bitter pill for Gary, who is honest to a fault.

"When we were little, if a store clerk gave twelve cents too much change, we had to drive back to return the money," says his daughter Laura Lewis. "He would do that just to teach us. Honesty was a huge value for him. And then this man who played on their baseball team had been stealing money."

Restitution was sought, but there wasn't much that could be redeemed. The travel agencies, a cottage, a Mercedes were all mortgaged. But there was a mahogany dining room suite and a set of silverware – engraved with the letter M, for the accountant's surname.

"Sometimes when we put out the silverware, guests will say, 'What's the M stand for?' I'll say, 'Mine!'" says Gary.

The dining room suite arrived when son Gord was 13 or 14 years old. He was helping his mother clean it and said, "You know, Mom, I really feel sorry for (the accountant) and the kids and his wife. That must be just terrible."

Eleanore peered down at him sternly and said, "You remember this: he almost killed your father with the worry and the stress that he put him through. So don't you ever feel sorry for a crook."

"OK, Mom," replied Gord.

Chapter 11
STEALING PHONE BOOKS

It happened every time.

Kim Schell would be getting ready to fly out to set up a new Lewiscraft store in a shopping mall somewhere in Canada. As manager of the store supervisors and someone with a sharp eye for retail design, Schell was always on site in the days before a new Lewiscraft opened.

Gerry Lewis would amble into her office.

"Are you going to the opening?"

"Yes, I am."

"What are you going to get for me?"

"A phone book."

"Atta-girl!"

When Schell returned from the opening a few days later, Gerry would be in her office like a shot.

"Got my book?"

"Yep, I got you the Yellow Pages and the White Pages."

Lewis, the patriarch of Lewiscraft, "wanted us to steal phone books wherever we went," remembers Schell. "We would steal them from hotel rooms or phone booths, wherever – but we always stole the phone books."

Gerry Lewis was, it seemed through the 1970s and 1980s, somewhat obsessed with phone books, city directories and postal code books.

After running a group of companies under the banner of Gerry Lewis Ltd. for twenty-five years after his father, founder Ed Lewis, died, he had officially retired in 1969. His only child, Gary, had taken over as president. But Mr. Lewis, as he was known to staff of the company most Canadians called Lewiscraft, wasn't quite ready for a retiree's life of golf and bridge.

For close to twenty-five more years, he still went into Lewiscraft's head office – initially on King Street West in downtown Toronto, later on

Gerry Lewis (left), late 1960s

Commander Boulevard in suburban Scarborough – every weekday (except for parts of the winter, when he was in Florida).

He wasn't there to interfere with his son's running of the business. In fact, even though he initially objected to Gary's decision to expand the business from a mail-order operation to a chain of retail stores, he didn't stand in the way of progress.

But Gerry Lewis did have a purpose, a valid reason for being in the office for eight hours every weekday.

He had to find new addresses for Lewiscraft's annual catalogues to be sent. And he did that by painstakingly poring over every page – heck, every line on every page – of phone books and other sources of addresses.

He would sit in his office with a ruler, a book, some coloured pens and a copy of the most recent mailing list. Once he found a name or an address that seemed worthy of receiving a catalogue and wasn't already on the list, he would underline it and write it out by hand. Then the new addresses would be handed over to an assistant who would ensure they got added to the mailing list.

One of Gerry Lewis's handwritten catalogue-distribution lists

His primary purpose was to ensure that every one of the institutions that were good customers for Lewiscraft's handicraft supplies – prisons, schools, churches, YMCA-YWCAs, summer camps and the like – was on the list. But he also marked scores of individual households, using methodology known only to him.

"He would go through and say, 'That sounds like a name that would most likely do crafts – we'll send him a catalogue. That sounds like a good name.' So he'd put that person on the list to get a catalogue," recalls Gary. "There was no science to it. Totally gut instinct. No scientific basis whatsoever.

"I had trouble trying to explain to him that the name McArthur could mean anything.

"The whole mailing list was being built on whether Dad liked your name."

It appears Gerry used a combination of postal books – officially known as "Post Office Householder Directories" – and phone books. A page cut out of a postal directory, tucked away in grandson Gord Lewis's archive of Lewiscraft memorabilia, describes the publications this way:

Mary Ohorodnyk, 1985

"Post Office Householder Directories are compiled for the Post Offices in a Federal Electoral District. They contain the names, addresses and occupations of the patrons served through these offices even though some of the patrons may reside in other Electoral Districts. Letter F before name indicates a French Speaking Householder."

The 145 directories available at that time could be purchased for five dollars per copy. Inscriptions in red ink on the page, probably written by Gerry Lewis, noted that all forty-one Ontario directories were on hand in May

1973, and wondered which book included the southwestern Ontario communities of Ailsa Craig and Lucan.

"He would write them out by hand," says Bruce Pearson, who served as a business adviser to both Gerry and Gary Lewis. "In some cases, he had addresses of places where they sent orders and he'd send one to the neighbour because he might do crafts, too.

"Writing them all out – the whole thing just boggles my mind."

Shirley Sano, who worked as head of design for the catalogues, says Lewis was pretty successful at guessing whether whoever lived at a particular address might become a profitable customer for Lewiscraft. He had none of the data that might be available today from Statistics Canada, although the postal directories did at least stipulate the occupation of each resident.

"Nowadays it's easy," Sano says, "but not back then. There were no computers to help him. Just churning out the names and addresses."

Gary's children have vivid memories of their grandfather with his phone books and pens and printouts of the previous mailing list spread across the desk.

"It really was his baby," says grand-daughter Lynda Henry. "He'd go through every phone book in the country. Page by page. Nobody has that kind of patience. He was blind in one eye, but he would just pore over those books."

Tricia Cadieux, who held several positions with Lewiscraft starting in the 1970s, recalls Gerry saying, "'Here's a few churches. This is where we've got to send a catalogue.' He was devout. That was his job."

Schell can still visualize Gerry scrutinizing the small type on those pages. "He'd have underlines and highlights in red. 'Institution, institution. Do these up for me.' And he always wanted to know what schools we contacted. Had to be in the know."

Gerry received postal books and other Lewiscraft correspondence by mail at his winter residence in Pompano Beach, Florida. Unfailingly frugal, he reused the heavy business envelopes, slicing them open and filling the insides with hand-printed lists of communities and addresses. One repurposed envelope in the family archive shows 185 municipalities in the vicinity of London, Ontario, from Adelaide to Zurich. Each is marked with a code: a red "x" means the postal book for that community is in hand, a blue "x" means "no postal," and a circled "x" means the community is "in Brantford area."

His obsession with the mailing list was not the only quirky personality trait demonstrated by Gerry Lewis in his 70s and 80s.

"He had nicknames for everybody," says Janet Campbell, who was a senior executive with Lewiscraft for close to twenty years. "He never called anybody by their name."

Campbell's future husband, fellow executive Bob Gatfield, says Lewis "would refer to somebody as 'so-and-so' and I'd be like, who the hell is that? Until I figured out the nickname."

It wasn't that he couldn't remember actual names. According to his son, Gerry had "the memory of an elephant." Nicknames were just something he liked to bestow on people.

Louise Chapdelaine was "Aunt Lou." Mary Ohorodnyk was his "downtown daughter." Kim Schell was "Sweetie McGoo" or "Miss Newmarket." (While most people called the retired president "Mr. Lewis," Schell was on cordial enough terms to get away with calling him "Grandpa.")

Gerry's nephew Alec Coutie, who worked in a senior role for many years, was "John."

"I said to him one day, 'Grandpa, why do you call Alec John?'" Schell remembers. "He said, 'When I first saw him as a baby, I said, I don't think he looks like an Alec. He should be named John.' Called him John all the time.

"When I first got to the office I didn't know who he was talking about. Alec would laugh and say, 'That's me.'"

Because he was blind in his right eye, Gerry discovered a route to the office that involved only right turns. Another quirk was his insistence on being accompanied at lunch every day by Mary Ohorodnyk, who was his secretary for nearly two decades and later filled the same role for Gary and Gord. Same little diner in a strip mall near the Commander Boulevard office.

"Every day," says colleague Mary Mackie. "You could set your watch by it."

Ohorodnyk – who always paid for her own lunch – has a vivid memory of the lunchtime ritual.

"Same food every day, sandwich cut in four. Always cut in four.

"He'd bring the phone books with him to the restaurant. It was mail order, mail order, mail order. He couldn't stop. That was his love."

With a bemused, affectionate smile, she adds: "Sometimes it would get to me and I'd say to Gary, 'Would you take your dad out for lunch today and give me a break!'"

Having joined the family business just before the Great Depression,

Gerry was the opposite of extravagant. In fact, he was constantly looking for ways to save money. But he could be generous as well. Ohorodnyk, who worked as his personal assistant at one point, recalls a time when she felt it was time to try working somewhere else.

"I had an interview with Sylvania Electric and they wanted to hire me. I went in the next day and said to Gerry, 'I've got another job offer. I think I might be going.' He says, 'You know, Mary, we can't. . . .' He was a little bit tight, you know. 'I can't give you anything right now, but the company is growing with the mail-order business.'

"He talked me into staying. I just couldn't leave him – even without a raise! A while later I wanted to buy a new car. I told Gerry and he said, 'How are you going to pay for it?' He took me down to his bank and co-signed the loan for me. And I thought, Geez, maybe it was the right thing to do to stay there."

Gerry himself stayed seventy years. He retired at age 90 and died two years later, in 1996.

Chapter 12

STACK IT HIGH AND WATCH 'EM BUY

Life was good in 1993 for Gary Lewis, the third-generation president of the family-owned Lewiscraft.

For the preceding two and a half decades, Lewis's company had continually expanded the number of craft supply stores it operated, from one in 1969 to seventy-eight by 1993.

Sales had also grown steadily and at times dramatically over that same period, from $1.6 million to $35 million annually. In that twenty-five-year span, year-over-year growth was in double digits eighteen times, and exceeded thirty per cent twice. Not once did revenue go down.

But a monster from across the border was about to change everything, forever, and not just for Lewiscraft.

In September of 1993, a Texas conglomerate made its first foray into Canada, opening two stores in the Toronto suburbs of Oakville and Burlington. And these weren't just any stores.

Michaels Stores Inc., operating under the Michaels brand name, was among the first companies to introduce to Canada a concept that has come to dominate retailing in this country: the stand-alone "superstore" anchored in a "power centre."

The idea was fairly simple: convert an old warehouse or slap up a new building – a "big box" – on vacant land near a major highway interchange so as to be accessible from a wide region. Avoid the high rents charged by shopping centres. Give yourself enough shelf space and inventory to sell on volume.

"Bix boxes, big parking lots and big shopping carts," is how retail analyst Len Kubas described it to the *Toronto Star* back in 1994. "Stack it high and watch 'em buy."

Within a year, big box stores – Future Shop, Price Club, National Sport,

Business Depot, Home Depot, even Pet Depot – were springing up all over the suburbs of Toronto and other large cities in Canada. Many were owned by U.S. outfits importing a concept that had already taken root down south.

The stores often resembled giant warehouses, with exposed pipes, utilitarian shelving, huge selections of merchandise and few of the traditional retail adornments.

They became known as "category killers" that would force existing stores to pick up their own game or face obliteration. By the time Wal-Mart, the world's largest retailer then and now, announced in January of 1994 that it was invading Canada by taking over 120 Woolco stores, some analysts had declared it game over.

Warehouse stores were "where all the action's going to be, from now to the end of the century," Ernst & Young retail consultant Art Good told a publication called *Profit*. Another consultant, John Winter, said simple revenue math – new model stacked up against old – dictated that "in about five years, half of the smaller retailers you see today may not be in business. It will be like Murder on the Orient Express – not one killer, but a whole lot of them."

Lewiscraft was one of the Canadian stores with a laser beam target on its chest. And the marksman in this case was Michaels.

Michaels Stores Inc. had gone public and started expanding beyond its home state of Texas in 1984. A decade later it had more than 500 stores.

Canada's two original Michaels stores in Oakville and Burlington, as well as five more that sprang up by the end of the company's first year here, were 20,000-square-foot behemoths. They sold essentially the same craft and art supplies that Lewiscraft stocked, but on a whopping scale. The typical Lewiscraft store looked quaintly puny by comparison: 1,800 to 2,000 square feet tucked inside a shopping mall.

"Everyone was really nervous when Michaels was coming, especially people who had shopped in the States and been in a Michaels," says Kim Schell, who managed Lewiscraft's store supervisors. "Because you're just like, oh crap, look at the size of this store."

"We can't compete with that."

Before Michaels arrived in Canada, Lewiscraft had the market more or less to itself in the eight provinces in which it operated. (Gary Lewis, who pushed the company into storefront retail in 1969, had chosen not to expand into Quebec, believing Lewiscraft could not keep prices low if it

To fend off Michaels' incursion from Texas, Lewiscraft emphasized its Canadian roots. From left, Gord, Gerry and Gary Lewis

had to replicate operations in French. He also stayed out of Prince Edward Island, concluding the market was simply too small.)

There were minor competitors scattered around the land: White Rose in Ontario, Fanny's Fabrics and Crafts Canada out west, mom-and-pop independents in some markets. But none could match Lewiscraft's combination of ubiquity (a store in virtually every city large enough to have a shopping mall), customer service (clerks who knew how to make pretty well any craft, and would happily teach you) and a vast array of merchandise (12,000 items either in stock or available by catalogue).

"Canada's craft store," however, was about to face its first serious competition. And a fellow Canadian was behind the threat.

Annette Verschuren, a business planner originally from Cape Breton, Nova Scotia, had worked in retail as head of a specialty men's furnishings chain called Den for Men. Eager to go into business for herself, she scoured the United States in search of store concepts that might appeal to Canadians. As recounted in a *Strategy* magazine piece in 1993, Verschuren settled on Michaels and presented its Texas-based owners with a business plan. They agreed to back the venture and take a majority stake.

Now there was something completely different for Lewiscraft to contend with. A store that seemed to embody "bigger is better." A store described by Verschuren as a destination unto itself.

Sales at Lewiscraft's store in Oakville declined after Michaels opened in that affluent town west of Toronto. White Rose felt the same pinch in Burlington, according to the Toronto Star.

"We aren't going to sit back and let them take the market from us," Gary Lewis said at the time. "We'll be butting heads, there's no question."

In fact, Lewis's strategy was to fight fire with fire. At almost exactly the same time Michaels opened its first two stores in Canada (the fall of 1993), Lewiscraft opened two superstores of its own: one at Crossroads Place in northwest Toronto and another in Oakville. Each was about 13,000 square feet, with 25,000 items in stock (compared with 35,000 to 40,000 at Michaels).

Lewiscraft had to change its business tactics substantially: introducing price guarantees and launching ad campaigns. When indoor malls were Canada's primary shopping destination, and only one craft store (a Lewiscraft) was in most of them, the company hadn't found it necessary to advertise much.

Now it was distributing colourful flyers and sending Gary's daughter Lynda onto mid-morning TV talk shows as the "face of Lewiscraft."

"When Michaels came in, I think part of our response was 'Screw them,'" remembers Gord Lewis, who rose through the organization over nine years to become vice-president of operations. "Dad's very competitive, so a little bit of 'You want to come in, we'll take you on.'"

Lewiscraft "did go into attack mode," confirms Gary.

Plans were hatched to open 20 to 30 stores of about 13,000 square feet – six to seven times bigger than the typical mall store.

Some Lewiscraft staff were initially enthusiastic about scaling up.

"One big store could carry everything, and that was kind of wow," remembers Louise Chapdelaine, who held a variety of positions with Lewiscraft, including oversight of mall outlets. "There was going to be lots of merchandise. Everybody was excited about it."

Lewiscraft's business model was ill-equipped to compete with Michaels, however.

Lewiscraft's prices were generally competitive, although Michaels could offer big discounts on some items bought in heavy volumes for sale in two countries. But a big difference was product selection – the relatively tiny Lewiscraft mall stores couldn't possibly stock as many items as Michaels had on its shelves. "The depth of their product was what killed our small stores," says Schell.

"We couldn't carry everything in our catalogue in the stores," adds Mary Gillis, who worked as assistant manager at the store in Oshawa, east of Toronto. "Quite often we had to special-order for people. That was a delay of a week or two. Or they could go to Michaels and get it right away."

One of the keys to Lewiscraft's success had always been its responsive customer service. Store managers and clerks would happily spend as much time as necessary helping customers learn how to complete a craft, or showing them how to solve a problem they had encountered on a project.

Although Verschuren (who later served as president of Home Depot's divisions in Canada and Asia) told *Strategy* that Michaels would offer a high level of customer service as well as product and project demonstrations, the reality turned out to be quite different. Michaels of Canada was not even remotely about customer relations; it was a business driven by speed and volume of sales.

"All the women who worked at Lewiscraft stores knew how to make crafts," remembers David Demchuk, a Lewiscraft fan who grew up as a dedicated crafter in Manitoba and for a period of time published a blog called *Knit Like a Man*. "They knew what to do and how to do it.

"You could go in and it was sort of like a Home Hardware type thing where the people have the knowledge to pass on to you, to repair something or do something that you want to do."

Michaels, by contrast, had clerks who were there simply to peddle product.

"I would never ask for help in a Michaels," Demchuk says. "Never. Some of those people may know some things, but the store is too huge, there's too much stock. They don't even know what they have, never mind how it works. Their thing is to sell you stuff. It's just where you go to get stuff.

"I wouldn't go into a Grand & Toy to learn how to write, and I wouldn't go into a Michaels to learn how to craft."

Tricia Cadieux, who managed several Lewiscraft stores and worked her way up to district manager by the early 1990s, says a Lewiscraft customer might say, "Can you help me with my knitting?" and a clerk would then spend half an hour explaining the stitches.

"One of the worst things was when people would go to places like Michaels and Wal-Mart to buy their yarn, then they'd come to us – they hadn't even bought the yarn from us – and they'd say, 'Can you help with this?' Because we were the people who talked to them and supplied the service and supplied the help. Our staff were like that."

Lewiscraft clerks "were giving all this great advice, and customers were still going down the street because they were 20 cents cheaper," says Mary Mackie, who worked in several Lewiscraft stores before becoming a buyer. "We did a lot of interviews with consumers and that was one of the big things that always came out of it. They'd say, 'Lewiscraft doesn't have as many whatevers as White Rose does, but I always go there if I have a problem or a question.'"

Cadieux, who left Lewiscraft a number of years after the company was sold by Gary Lewis, "didn't go into Michaels for years because it was like going to the enemy." Eventually, though, she applied for a job and went for an interview with Michaels.

She quickly discovered "I could never work for them. It was so NOT Lewiscraft. They had a limit on how much time you could spend with a customer. Everything was mapped out. It'll take you five minutes to take out the garbage. If you spend X amount of time with a customer, you'll be in trouble. That's how they worked."

Schell had a similar experience. "I worked at the Michaels up in Newmarket. I was there for maybe two months and I hated every second of it. I just thought, wow, they have no clue about their stock. They didn't know what they were selling.

"Lewiscraft to me always felt like family. Michaels, not even close."

Another difference was the type of crafts Michaels steered customers towards. Lewiscraft had "grown up" as a retailer by promoting a do-it-yourself ethos. Customers in the stores and ordering from the catalogues were encouraged to create crafts that were in some cases unashamedly homespun: creations made out of Popsicle sticks and pipe cleaners, for instance.

Michaels arrived just as Martha Stewart was all over TV preaching the virtues of making your home look as if it had been designed by professionals.

"Michaels was really trying to elevate crafting in its own way," says Demchuk. "Things didn't have that sort of homemade texture to them. It was all about doing things that emulate stuff you might buy in a store. Not stuff that's funky and original and connected with yourself.

"It was trying to push a more aspirational, high-end kind of feel. Michaels was aggressively middle- to upper-middle-class. And it was very much playing into a visual model and a creative model that was quite different from what Lewiscraft was doing.

"If you're going to have a wedding, half of which is do-it-yourself, that's the place you're going to go. I'm going to buy twenty-five things I need for the tables. I'm going to buy all my dried flowers. Here's where I can get all my ribbon. That's the kind of stuff it's about.

"Lewiscraft was never particularly about that. Lewiscraft was about projects and particular skills, rather than trying to achieve that sort of end result."

Faced with what Cadieux calls a "fast and furious" onslaught from Michaels, and to a lesser extent Wal-Mart, Lewiscraft moved quickly. The first step was to open its own superstores.

"If we were going to stay in the business, we had to start opening big stores," says Gary Lewis.

But, perhaps inevitably, something was lost: the intensely personal focus on the needs of each customer. Like Michaels, Lewiscraft's superstores were full of merchandise and employees, but lacked the personal touch that had been the chain's unique value proposition.

"It was not the same feel in the big store," says Chapdelaine. "It was so big, we couldn't be everywhere at the same time. You can't have staff in every aisle. You don't get that same connection with the customers. We tried to, but it was hard.

"Maybe we should have waited. We were ahead of our game and maybe that was a bit of a mistake."

Lewiscraft "didn't know how to fight the fire," Gary Lewis concedes with a sigh. "While we were really good at small stores, we didn't know how to run a big store.

"It's a different philosophy. We thought we could do it, but we were really not successful at it."

One of the problems was that superstores – Lewiscraft's and Michaels', for that matter – were simply too large to sell only craft supplies. "They filled it up with all kinds of other stuff," Janet Campbell says. Lewiscraft's chief operating officer through the 1980s, she left the company just as the war with Michaels was heating up.

One of the reasons the fight-fire-with-fire strategy failed, Mackie says, was that Lewiscraft endeavoured to "put too much sophistication in the stores.

Bob Gatfield, 1975

We were trying to make a small store into a big store, instead of making just a big store."

Attempting to compete with Michaels cost a lot of money. Superstores had to be set up and stocked, advertisements had to be created, lots of new staff had to be hired and trained, and the number of items for sale had to double. For a privately owned company without equity investors, this was a big stretch.

Bob Gatfield, who was then Lewiscraft's VP finance, notes that the company's steady expansion into shopping malls across Canada through the 1970s and '80s had been funded by revenue generated from operations. "We did it internally; we didn't use anybody's money. To take on Michaels and the big box stores would have taken a big buck. We couldn't have generated the cash."

Bruce Pearson, who was Gary Lewis's primary financial adviser and did substantial consulting work with other retailers, including Eaton's, adds that it's impossible to keep a retail business "fresh and alive" in the face of new competition without ready access to capital.

"The resources it takes for a retailer to change – it's a real user of cash," he says. "To change a store, just to remodel it to bring it into the next decade, costs millions. It's very, very expensive. The ones that are successful are corporations that have access to outside shareholders, outside cash.

"The speed with which Michaels came into Canada – this wasn't a slow road. The handwriting was on the wall pretty quickly."

Schell says she knew there was not "a hope in hell" for Lewiscraft when Michaels opened stores in small cities like Grande Prairie, Alberta, and Prince Rupert, British Columbia.

"We sort of didn't really know what to do," admits Campbell. "We tried a few things and they didn't work all that well. There was a lot of experimenting going on.

"We thought we could play their game, but we really couldn't."

Chapter 13
KNOW WHEN TO FOLD

The car pulled up to the house and parked, hidden from the front door.

Two men got out. They were wearing black jackets, black shirts, white ties.

Their chins and upper lips were puffed out. Their hair slicked back.

They were brandishing baseball bats.

They had arrived for a meeting of the family.

But this was no Mafia gathering. This was a meeting of the Lewis family: Gary, Eleanore, their children Lynda, Laura and Gord, and the kids' spouses (Lynda's husband, Peter Henry; Laura's husband, Len Giblin; and Gord's wife, Melinda Lewis).

The 1994 meeting would change the lives of all present.

Gary, the third-generation president of Lewiscraft – a company that had been in his family for eighty years – and Eleanore had called the group together to relay some difficult news.

After a year or so of deliberation, uncertainty and spiralling new expenses, Gary had finally reached a painful conclusion: it was time to sell the business.

As a result, Gord would not become the fourth Lewis to run the company. Lynda would no longer be the public face of Lewiscraft, in store flyers and on TV programs catering to women.

All members of the family would lose their personal connection to what Gary had built over the past twenty-five years: a retail brand adored by hundreds of thousands of Canadians.

For members of the Lewis family, it was so much more than that. The three children had been part of Lewiscraft all their lives. Paint had been poured into small Lewiscraft-branded jars in the basement of their home in northeast Toronto. Birthday parties for the girls had been highlighted by flower-making crafts using the company's Dip-it product. Eldest daughter Lynda had grown up to become a corporate buyer and spokesperson. Third-born Gord had supervised stores and managed operations.

As a senior Lewiscraft executive with an MBA, Gord was intimately familiar with the hard-headed analysis that had led his father to conclude that the best option was to sell – even though it would sever the Lewis family connection after three generations.

Gord, in fact, agreed that selling was the way to go. So he (with his brother-in-law as wingman) decided to add a sly touch of levity to what might otherwise have been a rather sombre occasion at Gary and Eleanore's Beacon Hall summer home in Aurora, north of Toronto.

"Peter and I dressed in black and slicked our hair back and put cotton in our mouths," Gord says. "We walked out of the car and came around the corner carrying baseball bats. And then we started talking like the Italian Mafia at a meeting of 'the family.'"

The flamboyant arrival broke the ice. Within five minutes, Gary and Eleanore had relayed the news. And their children (as well as Peter, whom Eleanore describes as "like our son anyway") had accepted and embraced the decision to sell the business.

The backdrop to the conversation was the arrival in Canada of a U.S.-originated retail phenomenon known as "big box stores." The wave of new competitors to existing retailers included a craft supplier, Michaels, hell-bent on building 20,000-square-foot superstores that would outstock and outprice the much smaller Lewiscraft stores inside shopping malls.

Even in the face of this powerful new threat, reaching the conclusion that it was time to sell had been a torturous process for Gary.

"I was hesitant at first because we were still making good profits," he recalls. "'Maybe one more year, one more year.'"

Adds Gord: "When everything is going well, this is the mistake that people make. They think it's going to go on forever. 'We're making money, everything seems to be OK, so why sell?'"

Janet Campbell, who had risen through the organization to become chief operating officer, says the White Rose chain had made an unsolicited overture to buy Lewiscraft. White Rose was a publicly traded company that operated nurseries; in the winter when plant sales were meagre, it competed with Lewiscraft to sell handicraft materials. Lewiscraft had

Members of the Lewis family: Lynda, Eleanore, Gord, Gary, Laura

always dominated the national craft market, and never perceived White Rose as much of a threat.

While he rejected White Rose's purchase bid, that proposition and the start of the big box wave seemed to trigger a period of intense soul-searching for Gary Lewis. He swung back and forth on whether it might be time to sell.

"'I'm going to sell; I'm not going to sell,'" Campbell recalled her boss saying. "He'd say, 'We're going to give it a go.' And then he'd say, 'No, maybe I'm wrong, I think we'd better sell it.'"

Frustrated over the lack of a decision, Campbell started to feel she herself might be impeding a clear conclusion, that Gary might be too loyal to sell the business out from under her.

"I thought to myself, 'I don't know how long I can keep doing this. I felt he had a better shot at the right decision if I wasn't there. I didn't really care which way he went but I just couldn't keep going back and forth, back and forth. So I decided I would leave.

"I said, 'I don't want to walk out but I think you'll find it easier if I'm not here.'"

Gary wasn't prepared for that. He urged her to stay six more months, and to keep quiet about the possibility he might sell the business. With some reluctance, Campbell agreed. And Gary kept trying to figure out what to do.

The alternatives to selling were stark and nasty: lose your own shirt trying to prop up a dwindling enterprise, or go into receivership and toss employees overboard with little or no severance.

While the business had been in the Lewis family for eighty-plus years, Gary also considered its employees part of his extended family. He couldn't bear the thought of abandoning them.

"The biggest concern was the 800 employees who were going to lose their jobs if they didn't sell to someone else," says Lynda. "Maybe either way it was going to die, but it had a better chance of living and continuing to support the people that had supported Lewiscraft all those years by being sold. So it was the best thing for everybody."

For the definitive analysis, Gary enlisted his son, who had moved up the ladder to become vice-president of operations.

"Gord and I went into hibernation for one or two days looking at the big stores. We did spreadsheets and computer programs, and we couldn't get the damn numbers to work. No matter what we did, we couldn't continue making money.

"Gord being an MBA, he was much better at numbers than I am. He could see that this wasn't going to work and the best thing to do was to get out. The best thing we could possibly do was leave."

The decision was financial, Gord remembers, but also deeply personal.

"My parents at that point were definitely comfortable, but it's not like they had money to burn," he says. "He was torn because it had been his life's work, essentially."

Bob Gatfield, who was vice-president of finance at Lewiscraft, says Bruce Pearson strongly encouraged Gary to sell. Pearson was Gary's most trusted adviser and a link, through his father, Harold Pearson (a long-time Lewiscraft director), to Gary's own father, Gerry Lewis, the company's second president.

"Bruce was there in the background telling Gary, 'Use your head. You've got to think about your future,'" remembers Gatfield.

Pearson, though, says Gary arrived at the eventual decision on his own.

Relieved: Eleanore and Gary on vacation after selling the company

"Gary is no dummy. He could see it coming. If you want to look reality in the face and say, 'Well, it's not going to happen,' then be my guest. But he knew what was going to happen and he knew he had to do something.

"To let it go into bankruptcy was certainly a hell of a lot worse than selling."

Aside from Gord and Bruce, there was one other trusted adviser for Gary to consult: his wife.

"Eleanore and I decided we were not going to be stupid and keep pouring everything we earned all our lives on a wishful thing to compete with a public company," he says. "White Rose was public, Michaels was public and we were a small, private company.

"We recognized that every company has a life cycle. Look at today – Eaton's are gone, Simpsons are gone, Robinson's are gone.

"There's a life cycle to any business. Our sales were starting to come down. We weren't getting the growth that we thought we would get. That's what sort of rang the bell in my head, that this thing is starting to slide and I don't know how to stop it.

"And then we've got Michaels coming in – the competition. Man, this is beyond me.

"If you sell at the wrong time, you're history. Eleanore and I felt, we can't see this thing lasting forever. We've had a good run and we aren't about to invest every cent that we've earned back into a losing ship. We're not going to keep watching it go.

"I decided to sell."

Gary claims the decision did not produce a lot of emotional turmoil. Eleanore begs to differ.

"He says the emotion didn't come into it, but how many sleepless nights did he have trying to come up with this decision? He talked a lot about Gord being in the business, Lynda being in the business. 'Am I going to be letting them down?' He had many sleepless nights."

Once the decision had been made, there were still hurdles to overcome. Not just finding a buyer – which took more than a year, with some dashed hopes along the way – but coming to terms with the idea emotionally. "It does take a bit of getting used to," Gary admits.

And then there was the burning need for the family to agree with the decision. So the meeting was arranged at Beacon Hall.

"The purpose of the family meeting was for Mom and Dad to say, 'Look, this is where we're at and we just want to make sure that everybody is onside with what we're trying to do, and why,'" Gord remembers. "The whole clan was involved. They were very up front with all of us, saying, 'We want everybody to be on the same page.' They literally asked for our opinion."

The business of the meeting took just a few minutes. Gary outlined his decision, and asked for the group's support.

"I told the family that Eleanore and I weren't prepared to continue to put everything, our whole life savings, into something we didn't think was going to survive. We tried to point out what we could see coming down and how the business had gone and what was likely to happen in the future.

"We weren't going to spend everything we had ever earned trying to keep this thing going for the sake of keeping it going."

"We didn't think there'd be any objection," says Eleanore. "The kids would all feel that it was really Gary's decision to make. Even though he asked their opinion, I think he was just being inclusive. They respected him too much to go against him. They wouldn't do that."

On board: Gerry Lewis (right, with Gord) supported his son's decision to sell the family business

Sure enough, the three children, along with Peter Henry, immediately agreed selling was the right decision.

"We all looked very objectively at the situation and it was a logical decision," Gord says. "It was just kind of an obvious conclusion. It was just so clearly the right thing.

"No one at that meeting was upset or crying. Dad did his little speech and then Lynda, Laura and I said something along the lines of, 'It's going to be the best thing for you and Mom.'"

Lynda Henry recalls her father saying, "Our family pockets are only so deep."

"All of us felt the same way," she says. "It was important for the family that my mom and dad were able to preserve equity for themselves, so they weren't going to be impoverished by allowing it to run itself into the ground.

"You have to do what you need to do. You can't be self-glorifying and think this has to go on forever just because it has your name on it. And I think all of us felt that because of Lewiscraft we were very fortunate.

"Gord, Laura and I had been given an incredible upbringing, not a spoiled upbringing but an incredible upbringing filled with lots of love and support. Selling was the right thing to do."

"I knew it wasn't easy coming up against these big box stores," remembers Laura, who had a commerce degree from Queen's University. "The writing was already on the wall and I just thought, 'Yeah, that's wise.'

"I was relieved in a way that they were going to do that. Because I think people can be foolish and prideful and end up losing everything. You have to be realistic."

The children on board, there was one more hurdle for Gary to overcome. He had to break the news to his father. Gerry Lewis had run the company from 1944 to 1969, built it into a mail-order powerhouse and continued going into the office for years after he handed the presidency to his son.

Gerry was finally retired now, in his 90s, but telling his father weighed on Gary nonetheless.

"He was really, really worried about that," recalls Lynda. "They'd had so much fun. Lewiscraft was a fun business to be in. The trade shows were fun; the people were wonderful.

"My grandfather said to him, 'Gary, it's not fun anymore. And when it's not fun, it's time to get out.'

"He was right – it wasn't fun."

Chapter 14
IN THE NICK OF TIME

"**W**ould you be interested in selling?"

"Yeah, we could possibly be interested in doing something."

With that nonchalant response to an unanticipated inquiry, Gary Lewis set a course to sell Lewiscraft, the company that had been in his family for more than eight decades.

It was a move he desperately wanted to make but had been unable to bring to fruition. Until the day Eddie Black, himself part of a family-owned business, approached Gary out of the blue.

While self-deprecating to a fault – he dismisses his stewardship of an iconic national brand by saying casually, "I sold beads and sequins" – Gary had learned one or two things in 25 years running the company. One of them was how to play with a poker face when the stakes are high.

"My dad said, 'It depends – maybe,'" recalls Gord Lewis, who was Lewiscraft's head of operations at the time.

Faced with new and growing competition from Michaels, the giant American craft supplies retailer that had crossed the border a couple of years earlier with plans of national domination, and after a great deal of back-and-forth deliberation, Gary had reached a painful but necessary conclusion. The third-generation president had decided it was time to sell the family business rather than watch it bleed to death.

Easier said than done, however. No buyers had emerged despite the company being shopped around for months. Prospective purchasers had quietly examined Lewiscraft's books, only to walk away without making offers.

One of them was Larry Stevenson, an MBA from Harvard who was running a consulting business and also, as he recalled to the *Financial Post* in 2008, looking for "a business to invest in, one that I could run myself."

He arrived one day to pore over Lewiscraft's financial statements and evaluate its prospects for future success.

"Larry was a pretty sharp guy," remembers Gary. "He came in and analyzed it, the history of the sales and all that, and he backed right off. He could read the numbers."

Stevenson decided instead to pursue the very same retail concept that was threatening to kill Lewiscraft: superstores. Rather than purchasing dozens of small craft outlets in shopping centres, he became founding chief executive officer of Chapters, creating a big-box chain that played a significant role in the demise of many small, independent booksellers across Canada.

Gary was left holding onto a company he believed had little chance of remaining profitable, and a great chance of draining his personal finances.

Then came the moment Gord calls "frickin' lucky – the luck of the Irish." While fretting over his next move, Gary received a phone call from Eddie Black. He was the grandson of another Eddie Black, who in 1930 had opened an appliance and radio store in Toronto. The elder Eddie's sons, Bill and Bob, had opened a specialty camera store in 1948 on St. Clair Avenue, calling it Eddie Black's Cameras.

By the early 1990s, Blacks Photo Corp. operated small outlets in many of the same shopping malls that housed Lewiscraft stores – probably side by side in some cases. (The original apostrophe in Black's was now gone; common business practice seen also with other famous brands such as Tim Hortons.)

In the days before digital cameras and smart phones capable of making high-resolution images that can be viewed on-screen and distributed instantly on Facebook or Instagram, Blacks was *the* place to go in Canada for snapshots. It processed film into prints and sold photo albums and knick-knacks.

The younger Eddie Black (son of Bill) had tried in 1993 to take over Blacks, which had been owned by Scott's Hospitality (KFC and Holiday Inn) since 1985. His purchase bid failed, and he instead joined a struggling ad agency, Saffer, as acting president. Saffer had devised the ubiquitous "Blacks is Photography" ad jingle but had since gone through receivership.

Two years later, Black "was looking for a new gig," remembers Gord.

"He said he was looking for a family type of business that was going through some change. He thought about Lewiscraft."

Gary, who knew Bill Black's brothers Barry and Bob, can't recall if he had ever met Eddie before being approached by him.

"He just phoned me up one day and wanted to come in and chat. I said OK.

"I guess he was looking for something to run. He obviously knew of me and Lewiscraft.

"When Eddie came into the office that day, I couldn't believe it."

There was finally a prospective buyer for Lewiscraft. Still, it wasn't as simple as saying Yes. While Black had the notion to buy the company, he didn't have the money.

"He had to go and find people to back him up, so I left the ball in his court," says Gary. "I showed him there was some interest, that if he could convince someone to invest, we would be receptive."

Black initially ran into the same resistance that Gary had when shopping the company around. The first group of investors Black brought in took a look at the books and decided against pursuing a deal.

"It really was quite stressful at times," Gary says. "It was on and off, on and off, on and off.

"It took forever."

After his first efforts to put together a deal failed, Black decided the case for business success would be based not on Lewiscraft's traditional model of 2,000-square-foot stores in shopping malls, but on going head to head with Michaels by building superstores 10 times that size.

This time he gained traction with a venture capital outfit called Westock. The key players were Bob Krembil, co-founder of Trimark Financial, and John Wilcox, who would become the operating partner.

"He did a lot of research and worked on a business plan and was able to put the plan together so it was believable to the guys," says Gary.

Asked how difficult it was to negotiate the sale of a business that had been in his family for three generations, Gary characteristically shrugs. "I don't recall that it was a big deal. I had Ernst & Young guiding me. They came up with what would be a proper value, so we weren't asking for the moon. It wasn't me that said a number, because the number that I had in my mind was about five times bigger than the number they wanted.

"We were able to find someone to buy it, which was just sheer luck, and then we got out. And that was the best thing that ever happened. Another year and we wouldn't have got out."

Gary has never disclosed the sale price but acknowledges that the deal included both cash and a tax-loss provision.

Gary Lewis in the Lewiscraft warehouse on Commander Boulevard in Scarborough

Before the sale could close, Gary had to confront the fact that selling would not only eliminate a family connection spanning eight decades – it would also scuttle his plans for Gord to become the fourth-generation president of Lewiscraft.

Gord, though, refused to cling to the notion that he should be given the reins. He was well aware of the company's dim financial prospects.

"I think 1994 was the first year the business actually lost money – the first year in its history. We knew Michaels was going to expand, so you didn't have to be a rocket scientist to figure out there were difficult times ahead.

"Dad and I had lots of conversations about it. Dad's mentality was, we've got to figure out what the right thing to do is. We're trying these superstores and they're bleeding us dry."

Unlike Gord, Gary did not have an MBA from the Ivey School at the University of Western Ontario. But he did have a business diploma from the then-Ryerson Polytechnic Institute, and he had studied best (and worst) business practices over the years through his membership in the Young Presidents' Organization.

One thing he had been keenly aware of from the start of his career was how family-owned enterprises often fall apart.

The *Harvard Business Review* described it in 2012 as "shirtsleeves to shirtsleeves in three generations: The propensity of family-owned enterprises to fail by the time the founder's grandchildren have taken charge."

The Review backed this aphorism with data suggesting seventy per cent of family-owned businesses are sold before the second generation gets a chance to take over, and only ten per cent remain active and privately held into a third generation. Business Week pegged a slightly higher success rate in 2010, reporting that about thirteen per cent of family businesses were successfully passed down to a third generation.

The business known to Canadians as Lewiscraft had begun in 1913 with Ed Lewis peddling leather to the Ontario shoe trade. It was taken over in 1944 by Ed's son Gerry, who emphasized the production of handicrafts sold through the mail. And then in 1969 Gerry's only child, Gary, became president and ignited a move into shopping mall retail that saw the company expand from a single store to nearly eighty in twenty-five years.

Gary didn't feel personally responsible for the potential decline of a once-thriving enterprise. It wasn't his fault that a big, well-financed predator had come into Canada. Nonetheless, he couldn't shake the feeling that he was embodying a grim tradition among family-owned businesses. (In the 1980s, Gary was a founding director of the Canadian Association of Family Enterprise.)

"Everybody says the third generation always screws up," Gary says. "First generation works at it, second generation gets it going and third generation buggers it up. And guess who was third generation? I was the third generation!"

Pearson, who also did some consulting work over the years for Eaton's, says families that carry a business across generations often can't come to grips with the idea that all good things come to an end.

"It's a very difficult thing to get right, whether you hold on too long. It's like giving up a birthright. I mean, it's like giving up part of your being. The family name and tradition. What the hell else did they talk about around Sunday lunch?

"They usually know what they should do; they just can't bring themselves to do it."

In this case, bringing himself to sell would mean no presidency for Gary's only son. But neither Gord nor his wife, Melinda, felt any tinge of regret about that.

"There was never any, 'I feel like he's selling this out from under me,'" says Gord. "Not for a second, not even an iota. He was always very conscious of recognizing that I was kind of the heir apparent. He was sort of looking at it as, 'If we sell, that's it.'

"I was on the side of, 'If we can sell it, then sell it. Don't be worrying about me – I'll be fine. You've got to make sure you can take care of you and Mom.' If my mom and dad are OK, that's good for me.

"I am cocky enough to think, I'm pretty smart, I've got a pretty good personality and I work hard so you know what, I'm going to be fine."

As it turned out, Gord didn't need to leave the business alongside his father. Because Eddie Black wanted him to stay involved, as an investor and an executive. Gord would own five per cent of the business, to ten per cent for Black and eighty-five per cent for the Westock investment group. Young Gord was about to get an education in the harsh realities of running a business under siege.

Chapter 15
BOYS' CLUB

The end of three generations of Lewis family connection to the company that bore its name came late in the afternoon of May 27, 1995: 4:30, to be precise.

That's when Gary Lewis – whose memory for dates and times is remarkable – signed the contract to sell his company to Westock Partners Inc., an investment group put together by Blacks Cameras scion Eddie Black.

The deal had been in the works for weeks, and members of the Lewis family – wife Eleanore, daughters Lynda and Laura, son Gord – were mentally prepared for it.

But emotional preparation was a different story. Knowing it was going to happen didn't make it any easier to face the end of a connection that had covered every day of life to that point for Gary and his three kids.

"Everybody was calling," Eleanore remembers, her eyes welling with tears. "Gord was phoning, Lynda was phoning, Laura was phoning to ask if the deal had gone through yet, if Dad was home yet. And finally about 5:30, Gary came in the side door.

"We both started to cry. We hugged and cried, and then we had a strong drink. Then we called the kids and told them what had happened."

Gary and Eleanore went for dinner at the nearby Toronto home of Lynda and her husband, Peter Henry.

Lynda weeps softly as she recalls the last day the Lewis family owned Lewiscraft.

"It had been a long process. You don't decide to put it on the market and it sells the next day. It was a long process, and I think every day my mom and dad had seen it become more and more clear that selling was the right thing to do.

"We had them over for dinner – just the four of us. We drank a little bit of wine and the incredible release from all that stress was immense. Within about three weeks it was as if (Dad) was ten years younger."

If the sale of Lewiscraft was emotionally draining for the Lewis family, it also had a dramatic impact on the lives of staff. An organization that had seemed like one big family was about to change.

What had been largely a girls' club was about to become a boys' club. Women who had spent their working lives at Lewiscraft and achieved senior positions were in for acute culture shock.

News of the sale did not come as a complete surprise to everyone when it was finally announced. While Gary had managed to keep only a few senior executives (and his family) in the loop, an active rumour mill existed.

"We got hints of it when Eddie Black appeared on the scene," remembers Shirley Sano, the art director who was responsible for the visual style of Lewiscraft, including catalogue design and signage. There was a "buzz" in the office, adds Mary Mackie, who was head of merchandising at the time. "It was pretty obvious what was coming down the pipe."

"It was a sad day, a scary day," says Louise Chapdelaine, who had risen from working in the warehouse to district manager in charge of a large group of stores. "A lot of things changed."

Gary's son Gord, now 30 and having worked with Lewiscraft in a variety of roles, was to remain with the company. He had accepted an offer to buy into the new ownership group and stay on the executive team.

"I wanted to be involved in it, and Eddie wanted me to be involved," Gord recalls. "The original business plan showed that my five per cent would be worth two million dollars in ten years. I said, 'Sign me up!'" Little did I know."

While Black had just a ten-per-cent stake in the business (with silent partners Bob Krembil and John Wilcox owning eighty-five per cent and Gord the other five), he was appointed the new president, and set out immediately to make some changes to combat a predatory competitor from Texas: Michaels, which billed itself as the Arts and Crafts Superstore.

Black – who could not be interviewed for this book before his death in 2015 – insisted on a different product mix, ordering truckloads of the picture frames that were a staple in Blacks stores. Sandra Massey, head of design in the company's "craft room" (where products were tested and new craft ideas developed) before and after Black's time as president, says he seemed to have the attitude that "anybody can buy crafts. If they can buy a camera, they can buy a craft.

"It doesn't work that way. No one who comes into a Lewiscraft store is there to buy picture frames."

Mackie, the head buyer, clashed with the new president.

"He wanted me to do things with merchandise that I just was not comfortable with," she says. "'We're going to take over the silk flower market. I want you to go out and buy a million dollars' worth of silk flowers.'

"I said, 'Do you have any idea what percentage of our sales are silk flowers? It's a dying market. There's Chinese stuff coming over here and they're selling them for thirty-nine cents a stem. Why do you want to chase that? It's stupid.'

"He didn't like being told off. He wasn't good with suggestions."

Black installed relatives in key roles.

"Eddie had his own people that he wanted in there," says Chapdelaine. "Some family members and some of the guys he used to work with at Blacks."

Black's mother-in-law apparently lived in Mexico during the winter; suddenly store shelves were stocked with sombreros and cactus figurines. Promotions offered the chance to win a trip to Mexico. (When Massey left the company several years later, she was presented with a scrapbook created by colleagues that described 1996 as "the year of the Mexican invasion.")

"I just thought, what are they thinking? What's up with this? This is not good," says Mona Kleperis, who had worked in the art department during Lewiscraft's heyday. She was no longer an employee but kept an eye on the stores. "There was just this decline."

Black "came in all bluster and larger than life, and then he started bringing in buyers from Blacks," says Kim Schell, who was manager of the store supervisors. "I thought, We're screwed. We are screwed.

"When he started bringing in buyers and all they bought was little frames, and sent his mother-in-law down to Mexico to buy little tchotchkes, I thought, Are you out of your freaking mind? You have no clue about the craft business."

Tricia Cadieux, who held several positions at Lewiscraft over the years, was managing the flagship store at Golden Mile Shopping Centre in

Scarborough at the time. She remembers receiving a room-sized stack of clay pots, "which really isn't Lewiscraft," purchased in Mexico.

"They were buying big massive deals – at one point we had a backroom just full of artificial flowers. Our backroom was huge and it was full to the ceiling. Like, hundreds of boxes of artificial flowers. They just bought very massively. You had to keep cutting it back in price because we had so much inventory."

Beyond a new approach to merchandise, the changes Black wrought also hit the culture of Lewiscraft. While Gord Lewis, operations manager Alec Coutie and finance head Bob Gatfield all held positions of authority under Gary Lewis, the company had largely been run by women, from Evelyn Hamill taking responsibility for mail order in the 1940s, through the modern era, when vice-president Janet Campbell and a bevy of other women played crucial roles at head office. (And of course the vast majority of store personnel had always been women.)

After Black took over as president, decisions were made mostly by men.

"It became a boys' club," says Mackie. "He changed it from a girls' club to a boys' club – totally. From the computer guy to the whole works – left the girls out of the meetings."

A company that to employees had always felt like one big happy family now became a place where doors were kept locked.

"We used to go out to the warehouse and say hi to all the people working there," Gary's daughter Lynda Henry remembers, "and if you needed something you'd just write down that you'd taken it.

"When the new owners came in, there were locked doors. People had to go through security checks before they left.

"I didn't even like going there after it had been sold. The whole feeling and environment and the culture had changed dramatically. I even have dreams about how awful it was – so cold and unfriendly. It was so not what we were."

"They constructed this whole security system," adds Gatfield. "Fenced in floor to ceiling – for a bag of goddamn beads?"

Black marginalized Gatfield, who had joined the company twenty years earlier as head of finance. "I had a contract that gave me an option of staying after the sale. When the new owners came in I stayed, for almost a year. It was a horrifying time. I was used to being involved and instead I was just left in my little office – 'Screw you, pal.' Just left to languish."

Black fired two long-serving senior managers, buyer Mary Mackie and art director Shirley Sano.

Chapdelaine got wind of the terminations ahead of time. She overheard a colleague in technical services mention that two employee discount tags had been de-activated: Mackie's and Sano's.

"He didn't think I would clue in that if they pulled their tags, then they were no longer employees. Well, Mary's my best friend. By coincidence she had called in sick that day. I called her and said, 'Expect it. It's coming.' I took the rest of the day off and went to her house."

Lewiscraft

Mackie had become frustrated enough with Black to consider quitting. "I had confronted him about two weeks before that. 'I've been here a long time and I feel I'm being excluded from what's going on. Totally excluded.' He said, 'Oh no, no, no.' I said, 'Oh yes, yes, yes.'"

"She had her letter of resignation ready to go," says Chapdelaine. "I said, 'Don't do it.' The more we talked about it, she agreed, 'Yeah, I'm getting it tomorrow.' So she was well prepared for it."

Sure enough, the next day Mackie and Sano were shown the door.

Massey was visiting one of the Toronto stores when the manager broke the news of their departure. "I was thinking, Am I next? I was in total shock."

The store manager, a rare male in a workforce dominated by women, tried to cheer her up. "I started to cry and he was trying to make me laugh. I said, 'I'll be living in a bus shelter,' and he said, 'Well, we'll put drapes around it. It'll be the best looking bus shelter there is.'

"That was a day you never forget. It was like the day the company died."

―――

For all he did to change corporate culture and clear out senior staff, Black's reign as CEO was plagued by financial strife. The company was bleeding cash almost from the moment the sale went through.

Westock had intended to go head-to-head against Michaels by opening fifteen to eighteen more superstores. Those expansion plans were scrapped in February of 1996, just nine months after the new owners had taken possession.

Two months after that, with revenues running twenty-two per cent behind projections set out in the business plan and the existing superstores losing money, the Toronto-Dominion Bank recommended that Westock put $2 million of new capital into the business. The ownership group agreed to cough up an additional $1 million; the bank in turn decreased Lewiscraft's line of credit by $1 million.

This reduction in credit followed closely on the heels of the company making payments for the three largest orders of the year – none of them traditional craft supplies: Mexico-related merchandise, floral and wood products.

The ensuing cash shortage meant many suppliers weren't being paid on time – they were "financing the inventory" – and consequently some of them stopped shipping merchandise to Lewiscraft.

"Fixed costs were going through the roof and the revenue wasn't keeping up," says Gord Lewis. "Revenue numbers were nowhere near what the projections had been.

"I was one of basically three people in the company who knew what was going on. The rest of the company had no idea: guys I'd been working with for nine years, suppliers we'd been building up relationships with.

"Lewiscraft was never late paying a bill, and suddenly now it's thirty days and then sixty days. I'm getting phone calls asking what's going on. Stores are calling saying, 'Can we reorder this?' And the mandate that came down to me was, 'Do not make any decisions.'

"That was the quote from Eddie. 'Do not make any decisions.' Do nothing.

"So I would go into work and look like I was busy, and do nothing. In hindsight, I should have played golf or just taken off somewhere. But I felt I still needed to go into the office."

The younger Lewis didn't stop pondering the business's prospects, however. In fact, believing that filing for bankruptcy was a virtual certainty, he expended considerable effort quietly drafting a plan to persuade new investors to take over the company and revive its fortunes.

The plan was laid out in a fifty-page document he completed in August 1996. *Lewiscraft: A Plan to Restructure* offers a fascinating glimpse into a company struggling to survive in the face of unprecedented, well-financed competition.

Handicrafts could still be a viable business proposition, Lewis's plan asserted: "Crafts are more popular now than ever."

Westock had embarked on an aggressive growth strategy requiring a significant capital infusion intended to increase sales over three years to $78 million (more than double its peak of $35.4 million in 1995, the last year of Gary Lewis's presidency).

The restructuring plan set out the challenge plainly and without emotion: "Lewiscraft's current position is that of being overbuilt for the projected sales revenues." The recent rise in popularity and awareness of crafting, combined with the incursion into Canada of Michaels, had created an "unrealistic increase" in supply, with square footage of retail space more than tripling between 1992 and '96.

Lewiscraft®

"There is at some point a finite demand (and) 1996 has identified the limit of the demand . . . a classic case of supply exceeding demand. Because of the excess supply, profits from all participants are below 'normal' and everyone is losing. . . . None of the big three (craft suppliers) made money last year."

Despite the walls appearing to collapse on the company, Gord Lewis reported that Lewiscraft was well positioned to return to profitability – by shrinking. His plan to restore the business to financial success was based on the following elements:

- Close the five superstores that had been opened over the past three years – their combined contribution to the bottom line in the previous fiscal year had been a net loss of $204,000
- Reduce the number of traditional stores in shopping malls from fifty-nine to the twenty to thirty that were "most profitable and most promising"
- Slash the number of head office personnel to twenty from forty-five; the CEO would be paid $120,000, four senior executives would

earn $50,000 each and the rest would make between $20,000 and $40,000 per year
- Reduce the number of items in inventory to 12,000 from the 45,000 needed to support a superstore-based operation

As evidence of how dramatically Lewiscraft's fortunes had turned for the worse, Lewis's report said the restructuring would reduce annual sales to $12 million – one-third of what they had been just one year earlier. Yet it pitched the business as still worth investing in:

> *Lewiscraft remains the most recognized name in Canadian crafts. There is demand for our products; our challenge is to identify our means, then live within them.*
>
> *Lewiscraft is a proven and known name in the Canadian craft market. Both customers and suppliers alike have enjoyed a constructive, positive relationship with the company over its 85-year history. The restructuring will cause interim pain to some suppliers and customers, however the longstanding relationship between the Lewis family, the company, the suppliers and the staff will allow the rebuilding.*
>
> *White Rose is on the verge of bankruptcy, Michaels is unhappy with Canadian results and Lewiscraft's profits come from its mall stores. There has always been and will continue to be a role for crafts in the malls. The role is changing and the opportunities are changing, however the opportunities are there. The company can return to profitable operations by quickly executing the strategic plan.*

One thing became clear shortly after Gord Lewis prepared his restructuring plan. Eddie Black would not be involved in any attempt to resuscitate Lewiscraft.

"I was driving, with one of the early car phones," Gord says. "I got a call from Eddie saying, 'We're getting fired today. Wilcox is coming in for this meeting and we're getting fired.'

"I wasn't surprised because you know it's circling the drain. I went in; they fired Eddie and didn't fire me. John brought me in and said, 'I'm the new president, Eddie's gone and we're carrying on.'"

On September 30, 1996, Toronto-Dominion Bank filed a petition to force the company into bankruptcy, saying Lewiscraft had defaulted on $4 million borrowed under its line of credit. In addition to the bank debt, another $5 million was owed, most of it to Westock.

That same day, Lewiscraft went to court to win protection from creditors. In announcing its intention to restructure, Lewiscraft said it had lost $4.5 million on sales of $32.6 million in the year ended April 30, 1996, compared with a loss of $1.2 million on sales of $35.4 million the previous year – the only year of Gary Lewis's tenure when the company failed to make a profit. Helped by a temporary infusion of $500,000 from Wilcox to restock inventories, the sixty-three remaining Lewiscraft stores stayed open while the business was restructured.

As principal investor, Wilcox triggered Lewiscraft's use of the Companies' Creditors Arrangement Act (CCAA), a federal law that allows struggling companies to avoid going bankrupt by establishing court-sanctioned plans to provide partial payment to those who are owed money. Lewiscraft would keep operating, with Wilcox as chief executive officer, and walk away from much of its debt – including what was owed to Westock itself.

Two months after TD Bank forced the issue, Wilcox's plan to buy the company out of bankruptcy was approved by an Ontario Court judge. The new sole shareholder of Lewiscraft was a Wilcox company known as Lance Cove Investments Inc., which agreed to invest $2.5 million in the business.

"Lewiscraft 1 was my dad's business," says Gord, outlining the machinations of the restructuring. "He sold it and the new owners (Westock) created Lewiscraft 2. That's what I owned five per cent of. I was trying to restructure it with my plan and did all I could, but couldn't make it happen. So it went through CCAA.

"All of the money was in the form of debt, and all the debt was callable. They created Lewiscraft 3 through the bankruptcy courts and it owned the debt on Lewiscraft 2. They called the debt, which Lewiscraft 2 couldn't pay, so Lewiscraft 2 went bankrupt, wiped out all the equity, and Lewiscraft 3 took over all the assets and there was no equity. I was told it was called a fifteen-minute bankruptcy."

The new Lewiscraft that emerged from the restructuring had to shrink, so some of the 500 or so employees were let go with virtually no notice or pay.

"In a CCAA restructuring you're able to fire people without any severance," Gord says. "The worst part of the whole thing was we had people who had worked with us for thirty years and got zero.

"You've got to tell them. I did some of it. I wasn't the 'hatchet man' but I was involved in a number of them.

"These people would be 50, 60 years old and they'd worked in a warehouse for thirty years. Where were they going to go? Nowhere. That was brutal. There were no winners in this. Along with the other investors, I lost a lot of money when they wiped out the equity.

"That was one of my first lessons about *pro forma* spreadsheets – they mean squat. You're trying to project out ten years. We didn't make the first year. And then eighteen months after that, they pulled the plug on the company.

"It was painful for everybody."

To help the restructured company keep operating, many mall owners across Canada agreed to reduce Lewiscraft's rent. "We are unique, and the landlords want to keep us in the malls," Sarah Kavanagh, Lewiscraft's chief financial officer after Gatfield left, told the Toronto Star in November 1996. "This is good news for Canadians trying to stick it out against the new competition."

In June of 1997, a little over two years after his father had sold the business, Gord Lewis announced he was leaving Lewiscraft. He became an investment consultant with Proteus Performance Management, a governance and investment consulting firm launched three years earlier by his brother-in-law, Peter Henry (Lynda's husband).

For the first time since Gord's great-grandfather Ed Lewis had gone into business for himself in 1913, there was no longer a Lewis involved in Lewiscraft.

The ouster of Black and arrival of Wilcox was "a hallelujah day," says Schell.

"It was terrible under Eddie. I'm looking around thinking I'm working with morons. It was just, get those idiots out of here.

"John came in, very strait-laced, very stern. John didn't laugh a lot. There wasn't a lot of fooling around."

Although the restructuring he led had kept the company alive and most of the stores open, Wilcox – who politely but firmly declined to be interviewed for this book – did not make many friends at first when he took over as CEO. He brought a hard edge to what under Gary Lewis had been a gentle, inclusive culture. While Gary acknowledges he was sometimes too soft-hearted to make necessary personnel moves, Wilcox apparently went to the other extreme.

"When Wilcox first came in there was quite a bit of shouting and yelling and very harsh kind of management, which was not the culture," Gord recalls. "Eddie needed to yell and scream if he wanted something done in a certain way. By the end of it he was doing a lot of this" (he raises his middle finger).

"By the end of my time there with Wilcox, he had figured out he didn't have to manage that way."

Wilcox took steps to repair the fraying culture. The boys' club that had emerged under Black came to an abrupt end. Wilcox restored two prominent women from the Gary Lewis era to positions of prominence: Chapdelaine became director of purchasing and Schell became director of operations.

"At first I thought, things are not good here, and one day I will come in and the door will be locked," says Chapdelaine. "But he came to see me and explained it all. He said, 'We're going into CCAA on Monday.' He was very honest about it. We were having trouble and he was hoping that this would resolve a lot of the problems. I admired him for that.

"He was tough to work for but had a heart of gold. He had a vision, and if you didn't agree with him, then hit the road – and I didn't blame him. It was his money. I think a lot of people didn't understand that about John. They thought the company had unlimited funds, and that's not the case."

The business limped along for nearly a decade, moving its head office from Commander Boulevard in Scarborough to less expensive quarters in Brampton around 2003. While some stores were closed because they couldn't make enough (or any) money, new locations were opened as well.

"We had good years and bad years," remembers Cadieux, who had managed a number of stores before becoming district manager for Toronto East and the Atlantic region. "John had to close a few stores because they were underperforming, in an attempt to kind of stem the bleeding.

"But we were still opening up new stores. He was always trying to get a better deal in a mall. Always trying to get the best location."

Thirty new stores were opened, bringing the total to ninety.

The only consistently profitable product line near the end was yarn, says Chapdelaine. "Everything else was really, really hard, and even the yarn business didn't have the best profit margin."

In January of 2006, Wilcox announced another effort at restructuring through CCAA proceedings. Up to ten stores would be closed quickly, he said in court documents. "The objective of management at this time will be to keep Lewiscraft operating and to close only those locations which are clearly not viable."

The company had more than 200 full-time employees and another 400 working part-time. It had posted a loss in six of the past eight years and was heading for another one in 2006. Its owner, the Wilcox-controlled Lance Cove Investments Inc., had advanced the business $11.7 million by June of 2005 and was owed $8.2 million.

Despite all that, Wilcox maintained in the bankruptcy court filing that he still believed in the business's potential.

"Various attempts by current management to improve the financial performance of Lewiscraft have proven unsuccessful," Wilcox wrote. "In my view, this does not mean that Lewiscraft is not a viable business, or that it cannot become profitable."

No one else saw it as a viable business, though.

A couple of months into the bankruptcy process, the assets were purchased by Bentley Leathers, which took Lewiscraft down market as a liquidation outlet before finally closing the stores.

"Bentley really didn't want the stores, they just wanted the locations," says Chapdelaine. "Bentley was buying all kinds of different items that nobody had any interest in. Fire sales; things were mouldy. Staff were afraid of getting sick from the mould. They were sitting with all kinds of stuff in the back room that nobody wanted."

Shelves were stocked with "very low-end merchandise," says Cadieux. "We had Niagara Falls figurines and ashtrays and a lot of knick-knacky things. The kind of stuff that Lewiscraft would never have sold in a million years. And it was all ninety-per-cent-off sale pricing, deals like that. Bentley brought in a lot of junk."

Bentley gradually shuttered the stores, although a few remained open well into 2007. Eventually, though, the Lewiscraft brand disappeared for good with the closing of the last remaining stores – just six years short of a century after Ed Lewis had gone into business for himself.

Almost a decade after it closed, bits and pieces of Lewiscraft still exist in dark corners of the Internet. Using the WABAC search engine, which archives old web pages, one can find product catalogues from the final years – in extremely plain design, including the now-reviled Comic Sans font. They show the company's slogan changed from "Your craft expert" in 2002-03 to "Canadian craft experts" in 2004.

After the final sale, some employees were fortunate enough to be retained by Bentley, but hundreds were simply let go without severance reflecting their service.

"There were a lot of tears," Cadieux says. "We had many managers and full- and part-time staff that had been with us for years and years and years. I got a chunk of money from what would have been put into the pension. That's all. There was no package, there was nothing at the end. It was rough."

Even though she lost her job and received no severance, Chapdelaine credits Wilcox for keeping the business going as long as he did.

"He cared about all the staff. He really did. That's what people didn't understand. They didn't think that John had a heart, but he did have a heart of gold. He cared very much about what was going to happen to everyone.

When he decided he really should sell it, he tried every which way to save everybody's job, or a lot of jobs."

Lynda Henry – who had made crafts using Lewiscraft Podgy as a kid, worked her first job at the Scarborough Town Centre store as a teenager and grew up to become the company's public face in TV shows and advertising flyers – recalls stumbling upon one of the last stores operating under the Lewiscraft banner. It was in an underground shopping plaza near the intersection of Yonge and Bloor streets in downtown Toronto.

"It was the saddest thing in the world. We had never had a store there, so I don't know why there was a store there but it had Lewiscraft signs – the old signs, brown and orange. And it was just this crap that was being sold off at discount.

"It was like a really cheap flea market kind of store. It was horrible. Just awful."

Chapter 16
SO LONG, FAREWELL

Gary Lewis sold Lewiscraft in 1995, but the final store operating under that banner did not close its doors until late summer or early fall in 2007.

Both Facebook and Twitter were in their infancy when the Lewiscraft brand disappeared from Canada's retail scene. Basic searches for "Lewiscraft" in March 2016 found about a hundred Facebook posts and roughly the same number of tweets, an infinitesimal fraction of the content generated by users of the two platforms over the past decade.

But before virtually everyone was connecting with one another through social media, Canada's crafters still found ways to communicate online. And within that small world of blogs and discussion forums, the demise of Lewiscraft was mourned.

On a forum at craftster.org, a user named "cat" shared her anguish on March 20, 2006:

> I am, but not for much longer, a manager at a Lewiscraft in Winnipeg. I have worked for the company for eighteen years, and never in a million years expected this. Every employee in Manitoba feels like they've received a swift kick to the head.... I have always strived on excellent customer service and had the best trained staff. Our knowledge about our product surpassed every other craft supplier, and that's what made us different. Our customers are grieving. We are grieving.

Just before Lewiscraft disappeared, but when it was clearly on its last legs, a blog named *The Girl From Auntie* had a lengthy post about the company.

(The blogger's identity cannot be discerned, and the blog seems to have had no new posts since 2010.)

> Lewiscraft owns a Canadian chain of craft stores . . . which, knitting-wise, carries about as respectable a range of knitting yarns as Michaels or the other big stores that are probably squeezing this company out. Despite my current yarn snob status, I have a soft spot for that store.
>
> The cotton yarn for my very first completed knit item (a self-designed sweater with eyelet detail and a cowl neck) came from Lewiscraft. . . .
>
> I think I've purged most, but not all, the Lewiscraft-purchased yarn from my stash by now, except for the odd ball or two that I pick up from time to time. . . . Other times I just go in and gawk at the novelty yarns and all the painting and foil-scraping kits designed to take the creativity out of crafting. . . . And I hope that in Lewiscraft's restructuring, the store closest to me makes enough money to avoid closure, because where else can someone who hates big-box chains go for Styrofoam balls?

Responding to a post titled "Lewiscraft is dead" on a blog called *Knit Like a Man*, "Nathalie" wrote this on July 10, 2006:

> When I learned to knit I went to Lewiscraft for advice on patterns and yarns, and if I ever had a problem with a project I was working on, they were there to help me sort it out. They knew me by name and would let me know what was new the moment I walked in the door . . . I'm going to miss the store and the ladies there.

A month later, responding to the same blog post, "Kathy" described herself as manager of a Lewiscraft store "way up north":

> It felt like my second home. . . . People still approach me to talk about those days and how service elsewhere is not there. . . . Hopefully one day another style of Lewiscraft store will come along. Till then, keep knitting and good luck to all who worked at the best store around, Lewiscraft.

Perhaps the most detailed – and balanced – online tribute came from the creator of the *Knit Like a Man* blog: David Demchuk. In addition to his now-defunct blog, Demchuk also wrote a column with the same name on the knitty.com website, where he described himself as having spent his youth, thanks to Lewiscraft, "festooned in beaded macramé belts and vests, bell-bottomed blue jeans 'embroidered' in glitter paint, murky tie-dyed t-shirts and denim jackets encrusted with patches and studs. Let's not even talk about what (my) bedroom looked like."

Demchuk's 2006 reminiscence, "Lewiscraft – A Good Night and a Fond Farewell," is excerpted here, with his permission.

> *It is a dark day for knitters and other crafters north of the 49th: Canadian craft store Lewiscraft has all but given up the ghost. After several years of struggling against mounting debt, the chain is selling off what's left of its stock at hugely slashed prices, closing its doors and shutting down its website – probably for good....*
>
> *While it was undeniably a vortex of fugliness at every major holiday, with the most violent visual offences reserved for Christmas and Halloween, you could find decent yarn and other basic craft supplies at decent prices if you did a little digging. Because the stores were located in major shopping centres (sometimes providing the only crafts presence in a given city's downtown area), it was the perfect place to duck in on a lunch hour to pick up an emergency crochet hook or some fabric glue. And let me tell you, some of those clerks had worked in those stores for a hundred years, and really knew their stuff.*
>
> *(Also, and this is just a "me" thing: because of their mall locations, and because the stores were so comprehensive, I could walk in as a guy and root around to my heart's content and no one would ever bat an eye. Even that one Halloween when I went up to a clerk and asked her what the difference was between organza and chiffon, it was like I was the 10th guy that day to ask that very question – and who knows, maybe I was.)*
>
> *To me, a large part of the problem is that Lewiscraft never appeared to make any great effort to change with the times. The resurgence of handicrafts over the last decade seemed to catch it completely by surprise, and few adjustments were made within the stores to reflect the tastes and interests of a new generation of crafters. Shopping at*

Lewiscraft was always a trip back to 1978 – except online, where it was a trip back to 1996. Sometimes this was cool in a campy sort of way, but often it was frustrating and disheartening.

If you could satisfy yourself with Patons and Bernat yarns, and Lily dishcloth cotton, Lewiscraft could be a great emergency stop for a stingy knitter – but despite knitting's return to prominence, the yarn section never grew in size or range, and was always hemmed in on all sides by a jungle of Styrofoam blocks and balls, garish plastic flowers, fantasy feathers, glittery "liquid embroidery" pens and paint-your-own-stained-glass kits.

Unsurprisingly, many younger/newer knitters avoided Lewiscraft in favour of higher-end (and higher quality) yarn boutiques, and suburban knitters found similar or better yarn at Walmart or Zellers. And, as Lewiscraft never did fully enter the world of the Internet in the way that other craft retailers did, online competition – both domestic and international – can only have made matters worse.

To many, it was the last bastion of the tacky and taste-challenged. Still, it's sad that Lewiscraft was unable to carve out a distinct and contemporary identity for itself at a time when the interest in handicrafts and do-it-yourself projects was soaring. And it's possible that no one would have known what to do with a hot-fresh-hip-young Lewiscraft – the brand might not have been able to withstand such a radical change.

I will miss you, fusty old Lewiscraft – but I hold out the hope that something more innovative and (ironically) creative will eventually rise in your place. Until then, good night and farewell. Canadian crafters everywhere hold their glue guns high to salute you.

Chapter 17
A Family Affair

Lewiscraft truly was a family operation.

Started by Ed Lewis in 1913, the business was taken over by his eldest son, Gerry, in 1944, a year after the death of the founder. Gerry, in turn, retired in 1969 and handed the reins to his only son, Gary.

All of Gerry's siblings – brothers Fred, Bill and Herb, and sisters Ethel and Ivy – held positions in the company at one time or another. Fred led the handicraft division in the 1940s. Herb, who was seen (at least by his colleague and sweetheart Evelyn Hamill) as the company's "future star," also worked in that division before he was killed in action during the Second World War.

Bill worked in a variety of jobs, mostly connected to the warehouse and the mail-order operation, into the 1980s, and became Gerry's unofficial chauffeur after the latter gave up driving.

Ivy worked as an office assistant in the 1930s and was responsible for hiring Miss Hamill, who went on to become a powerful figure in the organization. Ethel worked as Gerry's secretary in the 1950s.

Alec Coutie was a trusted colleague of his cousin Gary Lewis from the 1960s through the 1980s. He rose to become vice-president of operations.

And two of the three children of Gary and Eleanore Lewis played significant roles with Lewiscraft in the decade or so before the company was sold – but only after fulfilling Gary's requirement that they work at least two years for other companies. Both worked for department stores that have since (like Lewiscraft) gone out of business: Lynda for Eaton's and Gord for Robinson's.

Working somewhere other than Lewiscraft "was mandatory," says Lynda. "Two years' outside experience. Dad didn't want anybody looking at us and saying the only reason you're here is your family."

Beads and Sequins: The Lewiscraft Story

Three generations of Lewises: Rear from left, Fred, Ev, Herb, Bill, Ethel, Ivy, Gladys, Gerry. Front from left, Ed, Donny, Gary, Alice (undated)

(Coincidentally, Gord's wife, Melinda, also worked as a buyer for Eaton's, and at one point was responsible for purchasing craft supplies for the chain).

The Matriarch: Eleanore

One member of the family who was never officially on the payroll – but contributed to its success in other ways – was Gary's wife, Eleanore.

She used Lewiscraft products to make a few crafts over the years, "but Gary didn't want to see them in this house," she recalls. "He was sick of seeing them all the time. I wasn't that good anyway."

Asked if she ever worked for Lewiscraft, Eleanore says all she did was work in the basement of the family home, pouring paint from cans into small bottles. Was there a machine? "No – me. I was the machine."

Eleanore's main responsibility was raising three children. Like his father, Gary worked constantly: in the office all week and then in the store on King Street on Saturdays. "He raised the business and my mom raised the kids," says daughter Lynda Henry. "That was not atypical in the 1960s. My dad will say that the only reason the kids turned out half-decent was because of my mom."

Despite Gary's desire to keep his home a Lewiscraft-free zone, daughters Lynda and Laura were encouraged to apply their creativity to crafts. For Lynda's twelfth birthday, Eleanore decided attendees would make flowers using Dip-it, a chemical substance that was one of the Lewiscraft's most

popular products of the 1960s and '70s. You would take a piece of wire, shape it into a petal, then dip it into the chemical. Pull it out, let it dry and you had a plastic flower.

"I had all these little girls around the table making these Dip-it flowers," says a sheepish Eleanore. "We later found out it was highly toxic."

"It makes you high," adds Gary. "We sold tractor-trailer loads of that, and the damn stuff was toxic. We didn't know."

Although Lewiscraft employees often described the company as feeling like a family, most of them never saw Mrs. Lewis. She did not attend staff parties, and never accompanied Gary on visits to stores. And she was acutely aware that it would have been easy for Lewiscraft to take over the family's lives.

"When we would have family dinners," remembers daughter Laura, "sometimes my mom would be like, 'Please don't let this turn into a Lewiscraft board meeting.'"

The Uncle: Alec

Outside of Gary Lewis's own brood, there was one other family member who made a big impact on Lewiscraft during its modern era. Alec Coutie was Gary's cousin – the son of Alec Coutie, Sr., Gary's mother's brother.

Seven years older than Gary, Alec used to babysit his young cousin. He joined the company a year or two after Gary in the late 1950s, and stayed about thirty years. "Dad thought he should get Alec to come work with me," Gary says. "We spent all our working lives together."

"He was like my brother."

Through the 1960s, Alec and Gary increasingly took on significant managerial responsibility. Analysing the prospects for the mail-order business, they jointly concluded the company needed to open retail stores to accelerate its growth.

When Gary became president in 1969, Alec became his right-hand man, eventually working as vice-president of operations with responsibility for the stores and the warehouse. He would arrange for contractors to build stores.

When it was time to open a new store, Alec would be there pitching in – and making sure the bar in someone's room at night had olives he could munch on.

A tall, solidly built man, Alec was liked by everybody, says Louise Chapdelaine. A real gentleman, says Tricia Cadieux. One of the nicest people you could ever meet, says Mary Mackie: "Always happy and always smiling. He always kept everybody moving forward. Just a genuinely sweet man."

The Face of Lewiscraft: Lynda

Eldest daughter Lynda (who became Lynda Henry by marriage) was the public face of Lewiscraft for a few years in the 1990s. Billed as "Lynda Lewis of Lewiscraft," she appeared on Cityline and other TV shows oriented to homemakers, demonstrating crafts and promoting Lewiscraft products. When Lewiscraft opened big-box stores to compete head-to-head with Michaels, Lynda's face beamed out at prospective customers from the front of printed flyers.

Working for Lewiscraft for several years

partially fulfilled Lynda's childhood dreams, although she didn't rise quite as high up the ranks as she had foreseen. "When I was a kid, I always said I was going to run the company. I was either going to be a stewardess," she says with a wry smile, "or run Lewiscraft."

As a 15-year-old, Lynda worked at the Lewiscraft store in Scarborough Town Centre. Her manager, Tricia Cadieux, gave her no special treatment as the owner's daughter. Not long after she started, Lynda arrived for work – barely on time. Cadieux gave her a tongue-lashing. "She said, 'If you are starting at 5:30, you are here on the floor, apron on, ready to go.'"

She later did some dirty, repetitive jobs: washing shelves in the warehouse, filling huge bins with individual balls of yarn.

After her mandatory outside service at Eaton's, Lynda worked as a store manager and later as a buyer. But her most high-profile role was as the face of Lewiscraft.

"My face got plastered on the paraphernalia that was used for publicity. I would also do store presentations. It would be, 'Lynda Lewis will be at the Oakville store.' That terrified me because some people knew a lot more about the products than I did."

Lynda was "very good in front of the camera," says brother Gord. "And Lynda Lewis of Lewiscraft has a nice ring to it. In my mind we should have made more of that."

A Different Calling: Laura

Laura Lewis, middle child of Gary and Eleanore, was never very craft-minded.

Lynda, two years older, "is the artistic one in the family," Laura says. "She used to do different crafts and I would copy them. She would do candles and I would copy and do the same candle.

"She would let me. She was a nice big sister."

Still, she does remember completing some crafts over the years. "I did rug hooking – I made a little pillow and wall hangings. I did candle making and Dip-it, knitting and macramé.

"I did all this at a level two notches down from what Lynda would do. I would have fun; she would do it far more extensively and longer and do a more elaborate job."

Laura worked briefly at Lewiscraft, as a receptionist at head office when she was about 15. And later, while attending business school, she did a report for the company on pay equity, comparing different positions using set parameters to generate a pay grid.

Although she studied commerce at Queen's University, Laura was never inclined to run a company. She briefly established a small business selling knitting kits, "but I didn't like trying to make a profit off people. I felt bad.

"And I also didn't account for the fact that some people were bigger and needed more balls of wool, and some people were smaller. It was a very unfruitful business venture. I went bankrupt very quickly," she says with a laugh.

Rather than pursue a future with Lewiscraft as her siblings did, Laura studied and worked abroad. Volunteer work with medical practitioners in Haiti prompted her to return to school to study medicine, and she eventually established a family medical practice in Huntsville, north of Toronto.

Recently Laura has worked as executive director of Christine's Place, a pregnancy support centre in Huntsville. She practises medicine there and serves as executive director of the Canadian Association of Pregnancy Support Services. And she has travelled to India and Cambodia, educating women about how to avoid unwanted pregnancies and providing support for women in distress.

Knit Like a Man: Gord

Gary Lewis couldn't believe it. His third child and only son, Gord, had learned how to knit, and would frequently whip out his needles to work on a sweater – even in public.

"My dad said, 'You didn't do that on the plane, did you?'" says Gord's sister Lynda Henry.

A young man working his way up through the senior ranks of Lewiscraft – first as a district manager and eventually as vice-president of operations – Gord felt it behooved him to learn how to knit.

"I was definitely not interested in knitting, but yarn made up thirty per cent of our business. How is it credible that you're ignorant about thirty per cent of your business? So I learned how to knit.

"I knitted a sweater which I still have – but it did take me three years to complete."

Had Gary Lewis not sold Lewiscraft in 1995, Gord was likely to become the fourth-generation president of the company. But a senior role wasn't going to be just handed to him by his father.

153

"You had to earn your way, especially because the business at that point was pretty substantial. There were 500 to 600 people working there. He made the point very clear: 'There are too many people depending on me for their livelihood. I'm not going to just give something to somebody who's going to screw it all up, just because you're my son.' He didn't word it exactly like that, but pretty close."

Gord's earliest memory of Lewiscraft is going to the warehouse on King Street as a kid, getting into a bin and riding from floor to floor on a conveyor belt.

Like his sisters, he did some low-level work for Lewiscraft during high school. After working at Robinson's – initially as a sales associate in children's clothing – he earned an MBA, then returned to Lewiscraft as a district manager, and later national sales manager.

"As far as most people were concerned, I only got the job because I was the son. Totally unproven, I'm a boy in a totally female-oriented business, I haven't got any experience in the stores, I have no credibility.

"It was not easy because it was all women, they'd all been working together for a long time and now boom – you're all reporting to me. There were more than a few clashes.

"It took probably a couple of years before Mary Mackie, who was head of merchandising, said to me, 'When you first came in there were a lot of people that were very skeptical, but you've won over the lot of them.'"

"He became a real part of the group," says former colleague Louise Chapdelaine, "not just a member of the Lewis family. We learned a lot from him."

Gord was a stickler for small details. He insisted all managers and clerks wear their Lewiscraft-branded aprons in the stores. "It was the uniform. So when I was in the stores, first thing I would do was put the apron on."

Chapter 18
LOVE LETTERS

Canada's postal system played a key role in the story of Lewiscraft, from Gerry's use of postal directories to find new individuals and institutions for the catalogue mailing list to Gary's focus on retail because labour disputes at Canada Post frequently dried up the company's revenue stream.

Family members were also dedicated letter writers, sending news of the family and the business, and sometimes career advice, through the mails to one another.

Early in his career with Lewiscraft, Gary Lewis was sent on a trip to Kyoto, Japan, to explore business opportunities and broaden his horizons. He expressed gratitude to his father in a letter dated April 22, 1963.

> *Dear Dad,*
> *This trip is not all business but it is mostly for an education, and this is so true. . . . The tours, receptions etc., have been most interesting. . . .*
>
> *Two or three of the other men on the trip have expressed the same opinion as you have, and that is even if no business is accomplished it is a worthwhile investment as far as broadening one's knowledge is concerned. . . .*
>
> *I fully realize that a trip like this for someone my age is just about impossible unless you have special opportunities which only come once in a lifetime. This of course has become a dream come true, and only because of you.*

Words of course cannot do justice in a case like this but all I can say is Thank you.
Gary

Dr. Laura Lewis travelled widely during her formative years. She worked and studied in Bordeaux, France, volunteered with a medical team in Haiti and visited many other countries as a tourist before settling with her husband in Huntsville, Ontario, where she opened a family medical practice. She has a special interest in helping women and men facing unplanned pregnancies to make life-affirming choices, and in recent years has travelled to India and Cambodia to teach and minister to citizens about the value of life.

During her travels in the 1980s and '90s, she received many letters from her paternal grandfather, Gerry Lewis, each with nuggets about life back home.

July 6, 1980
Today is our 49th anniversary – how fortunate we are to be here to enjoy the success of you three (Laura, her sister, Lynda, and brother Gord). Grandmother and the guy she married are going to the Royal York for dinner today. It was there we spent our first night.

July 9, 1984
Yesterday being our 53rd wedding anniversary, we were at (Lynda's home). Just the five of us which included old Gord, who is a busy fellow. Last week he spent three days in Hamilton where a new store was opened, No. 40. His regular job is at the plant doing a bit of everything in the warehouse – and doing it well, and I think enjoying it. Especially pay day.

Plays golf when he can. And yesterday had an eighty round which I think makes him the present champ in your house. Also he seems to have the odd girlfriend from time to time.

You have no doubt heard that he has been accepted at Western, which adds something to the family college careers – Trent, Queen's, Western. Very good for any family to accomplish. And us of the old brigade are mighty proud. . . .

Undated, 1986
Lynda is doing very well in her shop. And next week she goes to train a new manager at Towne & Country store, which gives her replacement at Cumberland a chance to run the show there. Then in about six weeks she goes to Yorkdale to manage our new store there. So these moves all prove that she is doing a good job, which makes us all very proud.

Old Gord is working his heart out in the paint business, and I think he has surprised us all, the way he has accepted his responsibility. . . .

Aug. 18, 1991
Gord returned from Calgary and Lethbridge safely and was impressed with the Lewiscraft effort out that way. The young guy has been on the move a lot, returned from Vancouver where they opened the two new stores, the group involved to do the job comprised of twenty girls and old Gord. For the new stores they had hired seventeen new sales clerks who helped set up, and there were three from Toronto. You would think he would have had enough working with girls, at least for a while. But no, he has now started his holidays and is going to Nova Scotia with (future wife) Melinda – just for a week.

All in all, Gord's doing all that anyone would expect of him. He is going to be OK – and eventually a great help and satisfaction for his dad. And as always a delight for his mother and sisters. . . .

Hope you can read this. I'm a real senior citizen.

June 10, 1994
It's now over two years since (Gerry's wife) Glad left, and everybody here and elsewhere misses her. She was a friend to all. So the show must go on.

I think Gary and El go home (from Florida) next weekend. This trip has done them a lot of good. They are a wonderful couple, their company with one another is wonderful and now over thirty-five years, which is so unusual these days.

As you know, Laura, you and I are a part of a great family and are blessed.

I have actually retired and Gord now uses my office, which is as it should be. I'll not really be missed – I did little or nothing around there anyway, maybe got in the way.

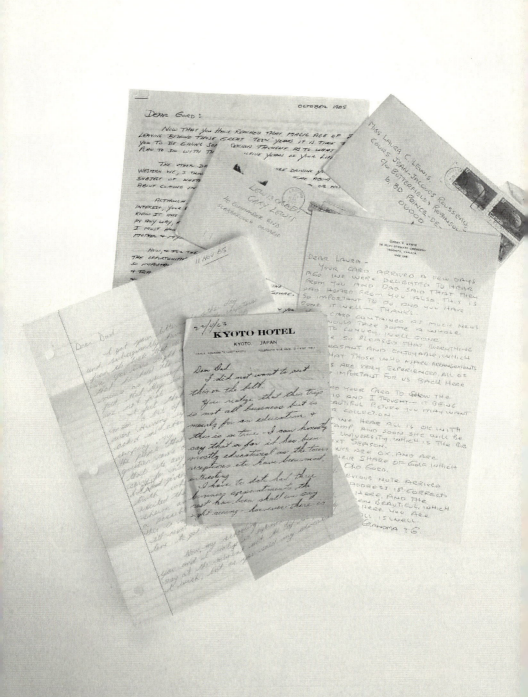

> It's good to hear the two bigger stores are doing OK. But business these days is tough going for most everyone, so we must be thankful for what we do have.
>
> Old Gord is doing a good job. He is the fourth generation in our little business, not bad in these days....

In 1985, Gary and Eleanore Lewis asked Gord – during a drive to the University of Western Ontario (now Western University), where he was pursuing an undergraduate degree – whether he would be interested in joining Lewiscraft when his studies were complete. This led to an exchange of letters between father and son.

> Dear Gord:
>
> Now that you have reached that magic age of 20, leaving behind those great "teen" years, it is time for you to be giving some serious thought as to what you plan to do with the productive years of your life.
>
> The other day while Mom and I were driving you to Western, we I think talked for the first time about the subject of whether you were really interested or not about coming into the "family business."
>
> Although I have felt for some time you may have some interest, your positive response was a most welcome sound. As you know it has never been my intention to force or pressure you in any way, as it is a decision that you and only you can make. I must, however, admit your decision is most gratifying to both Mother and myself.
>
> Now and for the next few years it is critical to capitalize on the opportunities to maximize your education, a fact which is so important for your future. It is after all this background and training that will enable you to become a flexible thinker and a person who is able to cope with the many complexities of business today and especially in the future.
>
> Speaking of the future, it is now when you should be considering your next step if you graduate in one and a half years with a BA. Some serious thought should be given as to whether you wish to go for an MBA. Although this is hard work at the time, it would, I know, put you in good standing for these years ahead.

Our company has been fortunate to grow over the past twenty-five-plus years. It is, however, still in its infancy as to its possibilities. Growth and prosperity only come from hard work (there is no free lunch). It has been just that from both Grampa and myself that will be providing the base for you, Lynda and Laura (should they also wish to join the company) to take the company that extra step.

Mind you, if the desire and the ability are not there by the time your generation comes on the scene, then of course stagnation will set in. It is this desire to build and to grow I hope each of you have, because this after all is where the true satisfaction and challenge of being in business really comes from.

While speaking of this you cannot overlook the amount of responsibility that will ultimately be placed on your shoulders. Not only will you be the fourth generation to be in the family business (that in itself is rather unique), but several hundreds of people will ultimately be depending on both sound and stable leadership of the company for their livelihood. Therefore, one cannot look at the future as totally a romantic and exciting opportunity, but must realize the responsibility this type of leadership carries with it. Therefore, the importance of getting as much education at this time of your life as you can possibly get....

I hope the foregoing pages will help give you some of my thoughts now that you have reached that threshold of your life where really the opportunities, the challenges, the fun and excitement are just beginning.

I am proud to be your father and I look forward to that day when we will be working together as a team.

Love, Dad

Dear Dad:
I felt that I owe you and Mom a bit of an apology. When we were driving up to London and you asked me about my interests in the company, my standard response to all the people that have asked me the same question came out. To them, I don't feel it's any of their business and I'm sorry for not saying how I really felt but instead giving

a weak response. In truth, when you asked me I became excited that finally you had shown an interest in having me be a possible part of the business, because this is my one goal in life, and though I'll never admit it to friends, etc., I'd love to get a chance to work for Lewiscraft.

Now, my schooling, which both you and I realize is extremely important, may at the moment not be of the quality I wish, but as you said my education will not end after a three-year BA. I feel that I'm a completely business-oriented person, and although my marks in philosophy don't flatter me, I feel I'd be a better candidate for the business school than many of the entrants. However, I think I may have a difficult time convincing the admissions committee of that. So, I plan (as long as you will be willing to support me financially) to further my education by either a possible MBA, maybe a CA, or both, or an alternate route, but I'm not done yet.

You know, sometimes I get down on myself after a bad mark, and not "up" enough after a good one (I do get some good ones!) but I guess I realize I'm human. . . . I need proper working conditions etc., but I am capable of good hard work when it's called for. And if the grade doesn't come in, to know that you're still proud of me makes all the difference.

So just in closing, thank you for all you have done for me, and I'm doing my best – you can tell Grandpa that!

Love,
Gord

Appendix
LEWISCRAFT'S HOMES

In the 94 years between Ed Lewis striking out on his own in service of the shoe trade and the closing of the final Lewiscraft store in 2007, the company laid claim to 10 Toronto-area addresses for its main operations.

50 Front Street East
A basement warehouse in the Frontwell Building, near Wellington Street, was the first location of Ed. R. Lewis Ltd. – Tanners & Leather Supplies.

21 Scott Street
Also a basement warehouse, this was located just around the corner from the original premises.

45 Front Street East
Lewis occupied both the basement and the third floor, across the street from the first location.

36 Wellington Street East
This move a block away in 1928 gave Lewis the luxury of two freight elevators.

284-286 King Street West →
With Toronto's leather trade no longer confined to a four-square-block area near the St. Lawrence Market, Lewis made a big move in 1934 to a

warehouse and office building in a grimy part of the downtown core. Ed. R. Lewis's rent was $65 a month. A modest retail store was also operated at this location.

8 Bathurst Street ↑
Just south of Old Fort York, this facility consisted of a group of shed-like buildings next to a railway siding. Gerry Lewis, the company's second president, described it in 1951 as "a glorified garage." Mary Ohorodnyk, who worked there starting in 1952, called it a "dinky little shack" with occasional visits from rats.

McMurchy Street, Brampton →
Gerry Lewis Ltd. purchased a tanning operation from Stacey Wagner Leather Co. in 1946. This

property consisted of a 16,000-square-foot tannery and "sludge-settling tanks" on five acres of land just west of Toronto. Lewiscraft got out of the tanning business and sold the property in 1965 to Bi-Way Stores.

284 King Street West

The company moved its main operation from Bathurst Street back to King Street in 1953. In addition to a warehouse, the building contained what was referred to as Lewiscraft Store No. 1 in what was becoming a more bustling part of Toronto's downtown. The company purchased the 42,000-square-foot, five-storey building near the corner of John Street in 1967. Looking directly south through his office window, Gary Lewis, Lewiscraft's third president, was able to monitor construction of the CN Tower. (That view would now be blocked by taller buildings that have sprung up on the south side of King Street.)

645 Yonge Street

Lewiscraft's first stand-alone retail store, this location operated in the late 1940s and early 1950s. Stores were also opened around the same time on Water Street in Saint John, New Brunswick, and on Graham Avenue in Winnipeg. The stores were declared a failure and closed by Gerry Lewis, and as a result Lewiscraft's only retail presence for nearly twenty years was at 284 King Street West in Toronto.

40 Commander Blvd., Scarborough

Lewiscraft's biggest operation was a modern warehouse and office facility in Toronto's eastern suburb. The company moved there in 1975, just as its expansion into retail stores was gaining traction. The King Street building

was sold to the Mirvish companies, which operated the Ed's Warehouse restaurant on the same block and later opened the Princess of Wales Theatre nearby.

321 Parkhurst Square, Brampton
About six years after the company was sold by Gary Lewis in 1995, its new owners, operating as Lewiscraft Corp., moved company headquarters to Brampton, west of Toronto.

ACKNOWLEDGEMENTS

This book could not have been written without the enthusiastic co-operation and participation of the Lewis family. I am deeply grateful to Gary and Eleanore Lewis, who sat for several lengthy interviews, as well as Lynda Henry, Laura Lewis and especially the project's initiator and sponsor, Gord Lewis. All cheerfully shared their memories and perspectives. They also opened their archives, providing me with valuable documentation of Lewiscraft's history and a treasure trove of potential illustrations.

I'm also thankful to the members of Lewiscraft's head office staff who agreed to be interviewed: Tricia Cadieux, the late Janet Campbell, Louise Chapdelaine, Bob Gatfield, Mona Kleperis, Mary Mackie, Sandra Massey, Mary Ohorodnyk, Shirley Sano and Kim Schell. To Mary Breen, Mary Gillis and Mark Mattin, who worked in Lewiscraft stores. To company adviser Bruce Pearson. And to dedicated crafters Angela Glover and David Demchuk. Thank you all for helping me understand the world of Lewiscraft.

My editor and writing coach, Don Gibb, has been a source of limitless wisdom and encouragement throughout this project, just as he has been for thousands of journalists across Canada over the past four decades.

Finally, my undying gratitude and love to my wife, Lauraine Woods, who has forgone travel adventures so I could continue to pursue my late-life passion for recounting big stories from bygone eras. In addition to being encouraging and loving, Lauraine has also provided inspiration as well as ideas that worked their way into the text.

October 2016

ABOUT THE AUTHOR

Paul Woods' first book, *Bouncing Book: From National Joke to Grey Cup Champs*, combined in-depth journalism with the passion of a diehard fan to tell the inside story of the 1983 Toronto Argonauts' rise to the championship of Canadian football after 31 years of futility and frustration.

A journalist and news executive, Woods spent most of his career at *Canadian Press*, the national news agency, as a reporter, editor, newsroom manager and Director of Human Resources. He has also taught journalism at Ryerson University, served as editorial consultant to the National Newspaper Awards and most recently worked as Executive Editor of the *Toronto Star*.

Woods lives with his wife, Lauraine in Burlington, Ontario, where they are fervently trying to master the ukulele.

Contact the author: paulwoods13@gmail.com

Photo overleaf: Lewiscraft national managers meeting, Donalda Club, 1988